100 REASONS TO CELEBRATE WELSH HISTORY

100 REASONS TO CELEBRATE WELSH HISTORY

VIRGINIA BUTLER AND CHRIS BUTLER

First published 2024

The History Press
97 St George's Place, Cheltenham,
Gloucestershire, GL50 3QB
www.thehistorypress.co.uk

© Chris and Virginia Butler, 2024

The right of Chris and Virginia Butler to be identified as
the Authors of this work has been asserted in accordance
with the Copyright, Designs and Patents Act 1988.

All rights reserved. No part of this book may be reprinted
or reproduced or utilised in any form or by any electronic,
mechanical or other means, now known or hereafter invented,
including photocopying and recording, or in any information
storage or retrieval system, without the permission in writing
from the Publishers.

British Library Cataloguing in Publication Data.
A catalogue record for this book is available from the British Library.

ISBN 978 1 80399 529 8

Typesetting and origination by The History Press
Printed and bound in Great Britain by TJ Books Limited, Padstow, Cornwall.

Trees for Life

CONTENTS

Prologues   9

Reason 1	15
Reason 2	17
Reason 3	18
Reason 4	20
Reason 5	22
Reason 6	23
Reason 7	26
Reason 8	29
Reason 9	30
Reason 10	32
Reason 11	34
Reason 12	36
Reason 13	38
Reason 14	41
Reason 15	43
Reason 16	45
Reason 17	46
Reason 18	47
Reason 19	48
Reason 20	50
Reason 21	51
Reason 22	53
Reason 23	55
Reason 24	57
Reason 25	59

Reason 26	61
Reason 27	63
Reason 28	65
Reason 29	66
Reason 30	68
Reason 31	70
Reason 32	71
Reason 33	73
Reason 34	75
Reason 35	79
Reason 36	81
Reason 37	82
Reason 38	86
Reason 39	88
Reason 40	90
Reason 41	92
Reason 42	94
Reason 43	98
Reason 44	99
Reason 45	100
Reason 46	102
Reason 47	104
Reason 48	106
Reason 49	107
Reason 50	109
Reason 51	111
Reason 52	113
Reason 53	118
Reason 54	120
Reason 55	122
Reason 56	123

Reason 57	126
Reason 58	128
Reason 59	129
Reason 60	132
Reason 61	134
Reason 62	136
Reason 63	137
Reason 64	138
Reason 65	139
Reason 66	140
Reason 67	142
Reason 68	143
Reason 69	144
Reason 70	146
Reason 71	148
Reason 72	151
Reason 73	153
Reason 74	155
Reason 75	157
Reason 76	159
Reason 77	161
Reason 78	162
Reason 79	163
Reason 80	165
Reason 81	166
Reason 82	168
Reason 83	176
Reason 84	181
Reason 85	183
Reason 86	184
Reason 87	185

Reason 88	187
Reason 89	189
Reason 90	192
Reason 91	194
Reason 92	196
Reason 93	200
Reason 94	201
Reason 95	203
Reason 96	205
Reason 97	207
Reason 98	208
Reason 99	209
Reason 100	211
Bibliography	213
Index	215

PROLOGUES

CHRIS'S JOURNEY

I was 6 years old when I had a troubling close encounter with the past. My father, who was a GP in Cardiff, took me on holiday to a farm owned by relatives in deepest rural Wales. It was not the complete lack of electricity there that threw me – the use of candles for lighting had a novelty value. The complete lack of toilet facilities – not even an outhouse – was more challenging.

Exposure to farmyard animals provoked my curiosity. I was staring at the cattle over a gate when I had my first alien encounter. A middle-aged man in ragged farmyard clothing came up to me and started talking to me. I could not understand a word he was saying. Because I did not respond, he started raising his voice and ended up shouting angrily at me. I had no idea – still have no idea – of what I had done wrong. I must have said something back but I don't remember what. Essentially, man and boy from the same country were looking at each other stunned by their mutual incomprehension. He had no English, and I had no Welsh.

Later in my school life, both primary and secondary, Welsh was taught poorly. The register of the language as taught was Biblical, not conversational. The textbooks we had were old, unappealing and falling apart. Welsh history in secondary school was part of a wider history curriculum, but Welsh history did not have some underlying uplifting theme such as in *Our Island Story* (written by Henrietta Marshall), which took us on a journey of gradual achievement, suffusing the global map with a glory that was coloured pink. The history of Wales seemed, in comparison, littered with squabbling princelings, defeats and disasters, punctuated by sublimely inconsequential events such as some guy stealing candles from a church. Just like my earlier encounter with the farmyard alien, the Welsh language and Welsh history left me uncomprehending of its meaning or purpose.

It was in my thirty-fourth year that I learned Welsh by the wlpan method. Now I could understand conversation, Welsh newspapers and television and I could read Welsh books – a new world beckoned. That was a start.

The process of the composition of this book taught me that there is a multiplicity of reasons to be proud of being Welsh – and more than 100 of them. Some facts may not seem so consequential: *The Natural History of Barbados* (published in 1750) by Griffith Hughes from Tywyn featured what he called 'The Forbidden Fruit' – it was the first description of the grapefruit. The descendants of a Welsh buccaneer, Robert Edwards, have a claim to a large part of Manhattan. The highest mountain in the world is named after Welshman George Everest, although it must be said he never saw the peak. However, other connections with Wales are truly momentous.

Witness the immense influence that people of a Welsh background had on the shaping and culture of the United States; witness the sporting achievements of Welsh people that are disproportionate to the Welsh contribution to world population numbers; remark on the enrichment of British culture through wondrous writing, acting, painting, poetry, singing and architecture – indeed, the fabric of the stately parts of London is often the product of Welsh talent. Running as a thread through all this is something that William Shakespeare put his finger on when he referred to Glendower as 'that great magician' – there is a romantic mysticism that seeps out from Celtic roots apparent even to blunt Saxons.

If English readers of this book appreciate better the contribution of Welsh people and culture to Britain and the world then it helps mutual understanding, and it is an antidote to the snooty, sneering attitude, evidenced in these pages, that Welsh people sometimes still encounter. In 2001, the TV presenter Anne Robinson called the Welsh 'irritating and annoying ... useless ... What are they for?' She merits a free copy of this book.

Welsh readers of this book may quibble about our choices to be proud of – fine, they could have compiled their own offerings – but they did not. Others will now realise the glories that Welsh people have contributed to the world. Perhaps Welsh history can be written in a way that does not dwell on perceived oppression, exploitation, grievance, rebellion and poverty (these are implicit in any national history), but rather in a way that thematically accompanies us on a journey of achievements, a recognition of the shining successes of the past, and an aspiration towards the sure triumphs of the future. Perhaps even I and the alien seven decades past can make our peace at last. I wish we could have communicated.

VIRGINIA'S JOURNEY

I was born in the mid-1960s. At that time, Cardiff, although the capital of Wales, was not a city that shouted about its Welshness. Cardiff was proud to have achieved recognition as the capital in 1955 but for the first half of the century it stood tall on being the biggest exporter of the best steam coal in the world. Cardiff had long been multicultural, with many nationalities living and working in Tiger Bay, in the shipping, steel and associated industries during the Industrial Revolution and beyond. The city then had few Welsh speakers and there were no Welsh language signs apart from place names, which very often were the anglicised version. However, I was aware of being Welsh from a very early age. My mother, although she had no Welsh DNA, was a very keen supporter of Welsh rugby and we would sit in in front of the television screaming for Gareth Edwards and Phil Bennett to perform their magic. Odd, isn't it, that English DNA can be transmuted by exposure to the Celtic spell? I knew my paternal grandparents spoke Welsh and that my grandfather's first language was Welsh, but a Welsh cultural side was missing from our upbringing. We were not chapel-goers and the National Eisteddfod was not something that we would have attended. I was taught no Welsh at school and minimal Welsh history. I had no friends that spoke Welsh. The nearest I got to learning any was finding a small booklet about basic Welsh in the attic of our house. The only nod that my primary school made to Welsh culture was having a school Eisteddfod on St David's Day complete with singing, poetry and dancing competitions but no Welsh.

We visited the National Museum of Wales but the collections would be displayed with little effort to set them in a Welsh cultural context. St Fagans Folk Museum has grown in its offering and it remains one of my favourite places to visit. It has expanded to explore Welsh history and culture in a more accessible way.

At the age of 11 I was sent to boarding school in Wiltshire and it seemed as if my Celtic roots might finally be erased. There was a small group of fellow pupils from Wales and we always enjoyed travelling home on the train together for the holidays. For me, entering the Severn Tunnel and seeing the now non-existent but then industrially majestic Llanwern Steel Works was an indication of being nearly home. Over time, our Welsh accents lost their lilt, often through the teasing by other pupils. Being in a school among some of the landed gentry of England, we adopted upper middle-class accents. For the next twenty years most people in my homeland thought I was English. University in London followed my schooling and after a further short time in the capital, I decided I wanted to return my Welsh roots and learn to live among my fellow Cymry. I was, in some ways, a fish out of water. I knew very few words in Welsh, very little Welsh history and was not well travelled in Wales. Joining BBC Wales in Cardiff made me realise there was so much more I needed to know about Wales. I longed to belong. Over the years, I started to educate myself in the history, politics and culture of the country that I loved to ensure I understood my heritage.

At the dawn of the new millennium in January 2000, I was travelling around India. In a small Italian restaurant on an unlit lane in Anjuna, Goa, I sat at a candle-lit table enjoying the convivial atmosphere. An elderly man was sharing my table as it was so busy. We started chatting and soon learned we were both from Cardiff. Marsden Preece was a director of the research centre at Cardiff Business School. Above the general hum of the chatter around me I caught the strains of some music in the background. I then realised it was Catatonia and the raspy tones of Cerys Matthews. I mentioned this to Marsden and he told me he had brought it out with him as he visits every year and he had given it to the restaurant. When the next track, 'International Velvet', started, I smiled and waited for the line 'Every day when I wake up I thank the Lord I'm Welsh'.

I hope that this book will help 'Awaken sleepy Wales' to its kaleidoscope of contributions to the world.

1

Because the contribution of Welsh people to science, culture, entertainment and society is regularly underplayed (usually by the English)

On 6 March 1993, the writer A.N. Wilson stated in London's *Evening Standard*, 'The Welsh have never made any significant contribution to any branch of knowledge, culture or entertainment. They have no architecture, no gastronomic tradition, no literature worthy of the name.' Strange to relate, then, that in his work, *After the Victorians*, published in 2005, the same author pays tribute to John Cowper Powys as a 'mystic genius that this craggily built Celt was'. Indeed, Powys was insistent on emphasising his Welsh descent through his father. He settled in Wales in 1935 and wrote the Welsh-themed novels *Owen Glendower* and *Porius*. He wrote in his 1934 autobiography, 'The idea of Wales and the idea of Welsh mythology went drumming on like an incantation through my tantalized soul.' Wilson, perhaps aware of his own inconsistency, concludes that Powys was 'surely the greatest English (*sic*) novelist of his generation'.

Much of the theme of this book revolves around the pride we have in the poets, famous singers and 'manly warriors' that Wales has produced. As the National Anthem states in its first verse:

Mae hen wlad fy nhadau yn annwyl i mi,
Gwlad beirdd a chantorion, enwogion o fri;
Ei gwrol ryfelwyr, gwladgarwyr tra mad,
Tros ryddid collasant eu gwaed.

The land of my fathers is dear to me,
Old land where poets and singers are honoured to be;
Its warring defenders so gallant and brave,
For freedom their life's blood they gave.

We have not confined our boundaries to famous Welsh poets, singers and soldiers. We have set our boundaries wider and wider still ...

2

Because a multi-talented Welsh star dominated British musical theatre from the mid-1930s to 1950

Exactly forty-two years before A.N. Wilson's magisterial pronouncement about the Welsh, 6 March 1951 marked the death of Ivor Novello. His biographer, Peter Noble, wrote of him, 'The great Welshman who brought more happiness to more people through his many gifts than possibly any other man of our century.'

Novello was born in Cowbridge Road East, Cardiff, in 1893, to Welsh-speaking parents. He was a great composer and songwriter of some fifty songs between 1910 and 1951, including 'Keep the Home Fires Burning' in 1914, which became the most popular song of the First World War. His song 'We'll Gather Lilacs' was a hit towards the end of the Second World War. He wrote eight popular musicals and took the romantic lead in several of them. According to *The Grove Dictionary of Music and Musicians*, Novello was 'until the advent of Andrew Lloyd Webber, the twentieth century's most consistently successful composer of British musicals'.

He starred in twenty-two films between 1921 and 1944. British and American readers of *Picturegoer* voted him their most popular star in 1928. He also acted in twenty plays between 1921 and 1944 and possessed an 'electrifying stage presence'. In sum, this one Welshman made a highly significant contribution to music, drama, cinema and theatre. Since 1956, the Ivor Novello Awards have been awarded annually recognising excellence in music writing.

3

Because the architect of the NHS was a Welsh statesman

In May 1929, Aneurin Bevan was elected Labour MP for Ebbw Vale, which he represented until his death in 1960. His father was a miner and died of an industrial disease, pneumoconiosis, leaving his family uncompensated. For someone who was largely self-educated, it was quite an achievement for Bevan to become the youngest member of Attlee's post-war Labour cabinet at the age of 47 and to create the NHS in circumstances of post-conflict austerity.

He designed the NHS to be comprehensive in scope, available to all and free at the time of need. It involved the nationalisation of all the 2,688 hospitals in Britain, some voluntary and some private. To achieve this massive reorganisation, he had to overcome deeply embedded vested interests, not least those represented by the doctors' union, the British Medical Association. It was a titanic struggle with harsh words being exchanged regularly. A letter in the *British Medical Journal*, for instance, accused him of being 'a complete and uncontrolled dictator'. Nevertheless, 5 July 1948 saw the opening of the doors of the National Health Service in Britain. It had taken only three years.

On his death in 1960, in a remarkably chivalrous turnaround, the *British Medical Journal* paid tribute to him as, 'the most brilliant Minister of Health this country has ever had'; and, to his 'force of character and brilliant powers of debate'. It hoped that future Ministers of Health would demonstrate similar 'imagination and flexibility of mind' – praise indeed for the lad who at the age of 13 had left school to go down a mine. The NHS is not without its criticisms and failures but lack of care because of inability to pay is not one of them. The service certainly needs someone with Bevan's drive and force of character to remedy its current problems.

Bevan's ministerial portfolio also covered housing and he played a major part in post-war reconstruction with his emphasis on council homes with gardens (later to be shamefully shifted to an emphasis on cheaper tower blocks).

Even the critic of Welsh achievements, A.N. Wilson, recognised the 'inborn genius' who brought about 'human betterment'. Bevan deserves, 'The laurel crown as the British politician who did the least harm and most good.'

4

Because Wales kept the light of Christianity during the Dark Ages

On 19 November 1967, the atheist English historian Simon Heffer wrote in the *Daily Mail*, 'It was lucky for the Welsh that they had the English to civilise them, an experiment they happily conducted with varying degrees of success over the next 7 centuries.' Heffer seems to have put the plough before the cow. Civilisation is normally strongly associated with the development of written communication and literature. Some of the earliest Welsh poetry attributed to the Welsh bard, Taliesin, originates in the sixth century. We have to wait until the fourteenth century before we reach the 'Father of English Literature', Geoffrey Chaucer.

Besides, the Angles and Saxons were pagans when they arrived marauding in Britain. The historian R.H. Hodgkin wrote, 'It was a consolation to [the Celts] to think that the invaders who had stolen their lands, and slain their clergy, were heading straight for hell-fire and an eternity of punishment.' Certainly, Welsh missionaries were active in the Dark Ages in Ireland, Scotland, Cornwall and France. They helped keep the flame of Christianity alive in Western Europe at a time when it was threatened by pagan Vikings, Saxons and others after the collapse of the Roman Empire. Indeed, this period is often called the 'Age of the Saints' in Wales. Terry Breverton lists more than 900 of them in *The Book of Welsh Saints*. Wikipedia lists 183 English saints.

Leading the Cymric community of saints we have St David (Dewi Sant), the Patron Saint of Wales. He founded a monastic community in the west of Pembrokeshire in the sixth century. William the Conqueror visited the site and recognised its immanent holiness. The Normans began building the cathedral that we know today soon after. David was canonised in the twelfth century by Pope Callixtus II. Callixtus decreed that two pilgrimages to St David's were considered to be worth a pilgrimage to Rome. Three pilgrimages to St David's were equivalent to a pilgrimage to Jerusalem, so persistent travellers to west Wales could wash themselves clean of all sin.

St Patrick's 'Confessio' states that he was born in Bannaven Taburniae, which many interpret as Banwen, near Ystradgynlais. The Patron Saint of Ireland was a Welshman.

In 2020, a BBC documentary showed that Llantwit Major in the Vale of Glamorgan was an important early centre of Celtic Christianity. Here was the first Christian College – 'Côr Tewdws' in honour of the Eastern Roman Emperor, Theodosius – in mainland Britain. Llantwit Major claims to be the site of the first university in Europe. At its height it boasted a remarkable number of students, some 2,000, among whom featured princes and saints. It had seven halls and 400 houses (come back, *Time Team*, see Reason 83). St David, St Patrick and the poet Taliesin are said to have spent some time there. The College was founded in AD 395 and it preserved tradition and faith until St Augustine came to re-establish Christianity and convert the Saxons in Britain in AD 597. It lasted hundreds of years until it was destroyed in a Viking raid in AD 987. It was rebuilt by the Normans after their conquest of Britain but as a more modest establishment.

5

Because a talented man of Welsh descent played a key role in founding Liberia as the first African Republic

Joseph Jenkins Roberts became the first President of Liberia in January 1848. He was the son of a Welsh planter in Norfolk, Virginia. His father set his mother, Amelia, free before he was born. She then married James Roberts, who was a businessman and brought up Joseph as his own. Joseph emigrated to Liberia in 1829, where the American Colonization Society was fostering the settlement of free black people and where he became a successful trader. In 1841, the society appointed him governor of the colony. In 1847, he encouraged the legislature to press for independence and after a referendum, Liberia duly declared itself independent and became the first African Republic. He saw Liberia as a refuge for persecuted black people and as a demonstration of African capabilities for sound self-governance. In 1848, on a diplomatic mission to the UK, he met Queen Victoria, and the UK was the first country in the world to recognise Liberia's independence. Roberts was re-elected president three more times and served eight years in all. He also served for fifteen years as a major general in the nation's army. He founded Liberia College, where he was professor of jurisprudence and international law. Monrovia, the capital of Liberia, is named after the US president of Welsh descent, James Monroe. Monrovia has Roberts International Airport named in honour of Joseph Roberts. His birthday, 15 March, is a national holiday in Liberia.

6

Because Wales is noted for its 'manly warriors'

Wales has the densest concentration of castles in the world. This is partly because successive English royal houses failed for hundreds of years to completely conquer and hold down the Welsh.

According to Wikipedia, there are twenty-five Welsh Victoria Cross winners and about 600 English winners. Proportionate to their respective populations in 2021, Wales boasts more medals than England. The Welsh national anthem praises Wales for its 'gwrol ryfelwyr' – 'manly warriors'. The Royal Welsh Regiment is kept at constant operational readiness, either to defend the mainland or to be sent on key missions abroad.

Without prejudice to those Victoria Cross winners whom we do not cover, let us briefly describe the exploits of six of them.

In 1916, Sergeant Major Frederick Barter from Cathays, Cardiff, was awarded the Victoria Cross for his bravery at the Battle of Festubert on the Western Front in May 1915. With seven other men of the Royal Welsh Fusiliers, he attacked German positions, severed eleven enemy mine leads with his clippers, peppered fleeing Germans with grenades and captured three enemy officers among a total bag of 102 prisoners, thus securing 500 yards of trench for the Allies. Barter was given a tremendous welcome in Cardiff when he returned. Modestly, he told the *Western Mail* that his exploits were, 'All in a day's work'. He was

Barter from Daniel Street, Cardiff, with his VC.

also to receive a Russian award for his bravery (the Cross of the Order of St George) and a Military Cross in Egypt in 1918 for conspicuous gallantry, but he eventually relinquished his commission as lieutenant in 1918 to join the Indian Army, where he was later to rise to the rank of captain.

On the same day, 31 July 1917, three Welsh soldiers each won the Victoria Cross. Corporal James Llewelyn Davies from Ogmore Vale was awarded the VC posthumously for conspicuous bravery during his attack on enemy lines in Polygon Wood, Belgium. That day, Sergeant Ivor Rees from Felinfoel attacked an enemy machine gun nest at Pilckem Ridge. He killed seven enemy, captured a machine gun and rounded up thirty prisoners. He survived the war. Sergeant Robert Bye from Pontypridd was also in action that day on Pilckem Ridge, showing utmost courage and devotion to duty clearing successive enemy blockhouses and capturing many prisoners. He survived the war, too.

Tasker Watkins was born in November 1918 in Nelson, the son of an engine driver. He joined the army as a humble private, but was rapidly commissioned to the rank of second lieutenant. Watkins won the Victoria Cross in August 1944 for extraordinary bravery in Normandy, where his actions as commanding officer saved the lives of at least half of his men. Watkins led a bayonet charge through booby-trapped fields under 'murderous' fire from fifty armed enemy infantry and then single-handedly took out a machine gun post to ensure the safety of his unit. He was the first Welsh soldier in the British army to win a VC in the Second World War . After the war, Watkins studied law, and rose to become Presiding Judge of the Wales and Chester Circuit, Lord Justice of Appeal,1983–93, and Deputy Chief Justice of England and Wales from 1988 until he retired in 1993.

7

Because Welsh archers repeatedly saved the English from humiliation in the Hundred Years' War and won the Battle of Agincourt, which led indirectly to the Tudors of Welsh descent seizing the crown

The Hundred Years' War between England and France lasted for 116 years (1337–1453). The war was effectively won by France, and English claims to French territory were emasculated. Two aspects of the conflict with Welsh connections are important to the flow of British history – the prowess of Welsh archers in saving England from complete humiliation; and, a twist in aristocratic genealogy that would ultimately lead to the Welsh family of Tudors coming to the throne of England.

On 26 August 1346, the English army led by King Edward III defeated a French army led by King Philip VI at the Battle of Crécy. About 15,000 men in the English army faced between 70,000 and 120,000 French soldiers. Serving with the English army were about 5,000 Welsh longbowmen. Longbows using heavy bodkin needle point arrows could penetrate plate armour at 246 yards and these archers could shoot at a rate of ten arrows a minute. The battle began with the longbowmen exchanging fire with the mercenary crossbowmen deployed by the French army. Since the longbowmen had a greater range and fired some three times more quickly than the crossbowmen, the longbow won out. The crossbowmen broke and fled. The subsequent cavalry charge by the French was hampered by the fleeing crossbowmen and muddy conditions on the battlefield. The longbowmen easily broke up the charge with their withering fire. At least two further French cavalry charges met the same fate, this time facing the additional obstacles of dead horses and riders littering the battlefield. The battle continued until the next day. Casualties on the English side were about forty in total; French losses may have been up to 30,000. It was a tremendous defeat for the French – victory was delivered to the English by the longbow, which probably originated in Wales, wielded mainly by superbly trained Welsh archers.

The Battle of Poitiers took place on 19 September 1356, between up to 40,000 in the French army and 12,000 in the English Army led by Edward, the Black Prince of Wales. Once again, the longbow wielded by English and Welsh archers was critical in winning the day for the Prince of Wales. The longbowmen began by suppressing the French crossbowmen with their slower rate of fire and less effective range. The Welsh archers changed tactics to target the less well-armoured rear of the French cavalry horses, and when they were able to close range this tactic proved successful. The butcher's bill was about 5,800 killed on the French side and forty on the English.

The Battle of Agincourt on 25 October 1415 was effectively the Triple Crown for the Welsh. Henry V, himself born in Monmouth, won an astounding victory over the French, who outnumbered the King's army by 2½:1. Five sixths of Henry's troops were longbowmen – many of them Welsh. One might think that the French would have learned strategic lessons from the Battle of Crécy nearly seventy years before – but no. The heavily armed French charged the English lines but were mown down by the archers in enfilade. Further waves of

French charges were broken up by the morass of dying men and horses and by showers of arrows. Four hundred of Henry's troops perished; some 6,000 French were killed.

As part of an attempted peace, Henry married Catherine of Valois, daughter of Charles VII, the King of France, in 1520. Henry died in 1522. While living at Windsor Castle, the widowed Catherine began a sexual relationship with a Welsh courtier, Owen Tudor, and she was pregnant with her first child by him in 1530. It was their direct descendant, Henry Tudor, Earl of Richmond, who was to seize the Crown of Richard III by violent revolution in 1485 and establish a new Welsh dynasty – the Tudors – to rule over both England and Wales.

8

Because by his brave example, one horribly injured Welsh soldier showed others how to triumph over adversity

Simon Weston was born in Caerphilly in 1961. He served with the Welsh Guards in the Falklands campaign and was bombed by an Argentine plane at Bluff Cove in June 1982. He suffered 46 per cent burns. He later said, 'My first encounter with a really low point was when they wheeled me into the transit hospital at RAF Lyneham and I passed my mother in the corridor and she said to my gran, "Oh mam, look at that poor boy" and I cried out, "Mam, it's me!"' He underwent years of reconstructive surgery, including more than ninety-six operations. His courage and charity work have been widely recognised. He was awarded an OBE in in June 1992, and later a CBE in the 2016 New Year Honours for charitable services. In 2004, he was named one of the top 100 Welsh heroes. In 2014, he was voted the UK's favourite hero. He has also written three autobiographies – one of which, *Walking Tall*, was number 1 in the bestselling list. Alongside these autobiographies, Weston has written four children's books. He says of himself, 'I am no longer defined simply by the terrible injuries that I received but instead by what I have achieved since.' He has three children by his wife, Lucy.

9

Because a premier hotel in Cardiff strangely became a ship that played a key role in winning the First World War

In 1883, the Angel Hotel opened up in Cardiff in the centre of town opposite Cardiff Castle to replace the esteemed old Cardiff Arms, which had effectively become a blockage to traffic. When it opened, it had seventy-six rooms fitted out in contemporary luxury. The hotel boasted its own stabling on Westgate Street. It was to become the swankiest hotel in town. Prime ministers and celebrities chose to stay here – stars with Welsh roots such as Ray Milland, Bette Davis and Shirley Bassey among them. Today, it is a hotel owned by the Cairn Group, but it is no longer the hottest place to stay.

The Cardiff HQ – Base 29 – of the US Navy set up in Cardiff on 1 October 1918 during the First World War, and they stayed here well into 1919. Why was the US Navy setting up its HQ in Cardiff? Welsh coal is the answer. The American Expeditionary Force (AEF) ran into supply difficulties in 1917. The army was running out of coal with all the consequential logistics problems. The lack of supply was partly due to the fact that the army was running the boats carrying coal stocks, and ships were taking a month to turn around and were arriving only

50 per cent full. The army was not great at running ships and had to call the US Navy in to help. By November 1918, sixty-five ships were involved shipping Welsh coal from south Wales ports to power the US Army and its supply lines.

The Cardiff HQ was based in the Angel Hotel – it occupied the entire building. The navy rechristened the hotel the *USS Chatinouka*. So, this grand old hotel made of brick became a landbound ship and US territory until 1919. Some 4,101 US enlisted personnel were involved in running the administration. In the four months to December 1918, 464,000 tons of Welsh coal were delivered to the AEF in France – an essential contribution to the winning of the First World War.

The Angel Hotel, Cardiff – US territory until 1919.

10

Because a Welsh businessman facilitated the 'double cross' system, effectively neutralising German espionage in the Second World War

In 1899, Arthur Owens was born in Pontardawe. Later in life he ran a company that supplied batteries to ships, was a contractor to the Royal Navy and was also well known to the German Navy in Kiel. In 1935, he presented himself at the German Embassy in Brussels and volunteered to spy for them, his story being that as a Welsh Nationalist he did not feel allegiance to the British state. They recruited him; as a travelling businessman with good naval connections he seemed to be of potential value. What they did not know was that their agent, 'JOHNNIE', was being monitored by MI5 through his illicit correspondence through Brussels. MI5 detained him and turned him on the first day of the war into their agent code-named 'SNOW'. MI5 gave him carefully concocted material to transmit to Germany by radio, and the trust he built up among them was such that he eventually effectively became their 'master spy' in Britain.

Owens was a somewhat louche character, motivated by sex and money, and his loyalties were perpetually suspect. However, it seems certain that MI5 got the better part of the deal. He was able to tip off MI5 about every German spy landing in Britain: they were caught and offered the choice of switching sides and feeding the Germans misinformation or the death penalty. Most chose to switch sides. By 1945, the British were running their 'double cross' system of some 120 agents funnelling duff information to Germany. MI5 made a profit from Owens's fake network of Welsh Nationalist spies, which the Germans paid for. The greatest success of the system was fooling Hitler that the D-Day landings would take place in the Pas de Calais rather than Normandy – possibly a war-winning coup in itself. Owens himself had earned some £13,850 from the Germans, worth over £1 million today. In 1948, he moved to a new life in Dublin, where he lived until 1976.

11

Because a Welsh tramp played a key role in defeating Nazism in Europe

Glyndwr Michael achieved great things but not during his life – he had been a penniless tramp. After his death, he played a pivotal role in defeating Nazism and winning the Second World War for the Allies. He was born in 1909 in Aberbargoed. He worked as a gardener and labourer but after his parents died he drifted to London, where he lived on the streets. He was found dying from rat poison in a warehouse in St Pancras. It was his very insignificance that made him valuable to British Military Intelligence. He was given a new identity as Major Martin of the Royal Marines. His body was dressed accordingly and given wallet fodder to chime with his new persona. He was taken by the submarine HMS *Seraph* to the coast of Spain and ejected in the sea near the port of Huelva. His body was picked up by a Spanish fisherman and taken ashore on 30 April 1943. The phony papers he was carrying then made their way – as had been hoped – to German intelligence. On 21 May 1943, a signal was intercepted showing that orders had been given to divert extra German military resources to Greece – the area where Glyndwr's papers had indicated that the Allies intended to invade. With the deception complete, the successful Allied invasion of Sicily went ahead on 10 July. The subsequent fall of Sicily eventually led to the invasion of the Italian mainland, the fall of Mussolini, and the liberated part of Italy joining the Allied side. Glyndwr is known as 'The Man Who Never Was' – 'Y dyn na fu erioed' – and the deception plan is known as Operation Mincemeat. Glyndwr is a war hero, buried in Huelva with full military honours. Never has such a Welsh man who achieved nothing in his life, achieved so much for the world after his death.

12

Because three inventions by Welsh people contributed significantly to defeating the Nazis in the Second World War

Edward George Bowen was born in Cockett, Swansea, in 1911, the son of a steelmaker. The lad was intelligent and won scholarships as a passport to a good education. He graduated with a first-class honours degree in physics from Swansea University. His postgraduate research involved X-rays. In 1935, he began working on the Radar Development Team under Robert Watson-Watt. The government hoped for a death ray but Watson-Watt had hopes of a detection system instead. Bowen was then granted his request to begin developing airborne radar. He solved various technical problems to deliver an airborne radar that could detect not only other aircraft but capital ships. By 1941, aircraft with airborne radar had shot down 100 enemy planes. Bowen's team moved to St Athan in south Wales and there he developed airborne radar capable of detecting enemy submarines. By April 1941, RAF Coastal Command was deploying 110 anti-submarine aircraft. 'Taffy' Bowen's contribution to the development of radar is acknowledged as a major factor in winning the Battle of Britain and the Battle of the Atlantic.

On 24 July 1943, Operation Gomorrah began. This was a series of large-scale bombing raids by the Allies on the important city of Hamburg. The operation was named after the city of Gomorrah, upon which God had rained fire and brimstone. Hamburg was a legitimate target as it contained shipyards, refineries, military industries and U-boat pens. The bombing lasted eight days and its effects were devastating. It was the heaviest air assault in the history of aerial warfare.

The Welsh connection is through Joan Curran, a Swansea girl, who gained an honours degree in physics at Cambridge, before women could be awarded a degree officially. At the Telecommunications Research Establishment, Swanage, she worked on the use of tinfoil strips known as 'Operation Window' as a means of confusing enemy radar, and this resulted in much lower losses of Allied bombers during the Hamburg raid. It was also used successfully during Operation Taxable in 1944 to confuse the Germans during D-Day. Joan also played a part in developing the proximity fuze, which formed an important role in shooting down V-1 flying bombs later in the war, and she also collaborated on the Manhattan Project to develop a nuclear bomb. In sum, this highly intelligent Welsh woman contributed mightily to the defeat of fascism.

David Brunt was born in 1886 in Staylittle, Montgomeryshire. Between 1936 and 1939, he contributed to a theoretical understanding of fog dispersal, information used in the development of the FIDO system, which was to assist many an Allied plane to land safely in the Second World War. After the war he became the first full-time Professor of Meteorology at Imperial College. Brunt is otherwise known as 'the Father of Meteorology'. He has an ice shelf named after him in Antarctica.

13

Because a Welsh scriptwriter revolutionised science fiction for baby boomers and Generation X; and because a Welsh executive producer revived the genre with successful spinoffs

Welsh writer Terry Nation was born in Llandaff in Cardiff in 1930. He began his career as a comedy scriptwriter working for famous comedians such as Stanley Baxter, Frankie Howerd, Eric Sykes, Harry Worth, Terry Scott and Tony Hancock. His biggest break was in 1963 when he was asked to work on *Doctor Who* scripts – indeed, he worked on sixty-two episodes. He created the Dalek, a squid-like being in a state of permanent petulance and conveying itself around inside a gliding metal box fitted with a death ray. These death rays are used regularly because Daleks think themselves superior to all other creatures, who must be exterminated. These determined robotic death-dealers were described by Alan Roderick, another Welsh writer, as 'pepperpots of the fascist variety'. Readers of sci-fi magazine *SFX* voted Daleks the all-time greatest monsters in 2010.

In 1978, the BBC first aired the cult classic science fiction programme *Blake's 7*, which was conceived and scripted by Nation and ran for four series. Low budget though it was, it had an audience of up to 10 million in the UK, and the series was rebroadcast in twenty-five other countries. The main character, Roj Blake, was played by Welshman Gareth Thomas, who was born in Aberystwyth in 1945, and who was brother to Harvey Thomas, PR guru to Margaret Thatcher, British prime minister between 1979 and 1991. Blake played a charismatic anarchist leading a band of seven in rebellion against the authoritarian Terran Federation, an intergalactic cabal that used mass surveillance, deep state repression, control of the media, fake news, show trials and enforced pharmaceuticals to control and exploit its citizens. Blake was betrayed and shot by his second in command, Avon. Nation wrote eighteen episodes of *Blake's 7*, leaving his fans longing for more. However, Nation died in 1997 while he was planning a fifth series.

To be the creative mind behind two multi-series TV sci-fi block-busters is a resounding achievement. The common theme was the struggle of sometimes flawed human individuals battling to retain their freedom against aggressive and evil cabals.

Russell T. Davies was born in April 1963 in Swansea. He became a screenwriter and TV producer. *Dark Season*, the BBC series he created, was the breakthrough for actress Kate Winslet in 1991. From the 1990s, he was lobbying the BBC to revive the *Doctor Who* series in an updated format more suited to the twenty-first century. Persistence paid off. Between 2005 and 2010, he wrote and produced thirty-one episodes. In 2005, *Doctor Who* won him two television awards: Best Drama Award and Pioneer Audience Award. In 2023, he returned to the show as executive producer and head writer. Davies also created a TV spinoff of *Doctor Who*, *Torchwood*, which ran for four seasons between 2006 and 2011. The series follows a team based in the Torchwood Institute in Cardiff that hunts aliens who have infiltrated the city via a time rift. The series won several awards. Davies created another spinoff, *The Sarah Jane Adventures*. It ran for fifty-three episodes over five series from 2007 to 2011.

14

Because three Welsh scientists have won Nobel Prizes

A Welshman discovered that we live in a matrix. Brian Josephson was born in Cardiff in 1940. He developed an aptitude for physics when he attended Cardiff High School for Boys. He went to Trinity College, Cambridge, where he gained a PhD in physics and became professor emeritus. He was only 22 when he undertook research on quantum tunnelling and superconductivity. He discovered a phenomenon known as the 'Josephson Effect', which won him the Nobel Prize for Physics in 1973. The Effect is concerned with supercurrents tunnelling through thin barriers. This discovery heralded important advances in technology including superconducting quantum interference devices, Squids, which are used to make sensitive geological measurements. Medicine and computing benefited too; IBM built a prototype computer in 1980 that promised to be 100 times faster than its existing mainframe. His work won many other awards. He established the Mind-Matter Unification Project at the Cavendish Laboratory in Cambridge to explore possible relationships between quantum physics and consciousness. He believes that prior to the Big Bang, a more elementary form of life evolved at the level of ideas and found a way of organising energy to create the physical universe and to make fruitful use of the matter inside this universe. This form of life, represented in human consciousness, observes, and by observing creates, the reality that we perceive around us, and consciousness can help evolve that reality. Josephson's quantum physics is indeed a challenge to traditionally received perceptions, but most of us are not quantum physicists. Broadly speaking, quantum physicists think there is a 50 per cent chance that we live in a matrix created by a consciousness, so Josephson is not alone in his assertion.

A primary school teacher told the mother of a young Swansea lad that he would never be successful. However, this boy, Clive Granger, born in 1934 studied mathematics and economics at Nottingham University. His career took him to a Nobel Prize in Economic Sciences in 2003 for his work on the concept of cointegration – a concept so complex it is difficult to explain but essentially it could identify factors that were causative rather than simply correlated. This improved forecasting and data modelling. He retired in 2003 to confront problems that hitherto were insoluble. Granger was knighted in 2005.

In 2007, Sir Martin Evans, a Welsh biologist, was awarded the Nobel Prize for Medicine. It was awarded for his 'series of ground-breaking discoveries concerning embryonic stem cells and DNA recombination in mammals'. The Nobel Assembly added, 'Its impact on the understanding of gene function and its benefits to mankind will continue to increase over many years to come.' Sir Martin essentially discovered embryonic stem cells that nowadays are used in a wide range of medical scenarios, and there is promise that further research will endow humanity with new, effective treatments. In 1999, he became Professor of Mammalian Genetics and Director of the School of Biosciences at Cardiff University – the institution where he later became President, then Chancellor.

15

Because without two key Welsh inventions, the world as we know it would stop moving

Where would we be without ball bearings? Computer fans use ball bearings. They are key features of aircraft and automobiles that help them run efficiently. Washing machines, vacuum cleaners, bicycles, trains and many items of medical equipment depend on ball bearings.

Philip Vaughan, an iron master from Carmarthen, was the first man to patent a first ball bearing mechanism. He described how iron balls running in a groove between the wheel and the axle would reduce friction in his patent of 1794. His first use of his invention was in carriage wheels. His technology is essential to many modern rotating machines.

William Robert Grove was born in Swansea in 1811. He was later to be hailed as 'the Welsh Tesla' by *Herald Wales*. He studied Classics at Brasenose College, Oxford, and was called to the Bar at Lincoln's Inn in 1832. He became a judge in 1872. However, it is not his legal career, as distinguished as it was, that gives him his proud claim to fame but his achievements as a scientist and inventor. Specifically, in 1839 he developed a new form of electric cell – the Grove Cell. It was powered by two electrodes, one zinc and one platinum, bathed in acids but separated by a porous ceramic plate. Grove presented his discoveries at the Royal Institution on 13 March 1840. The presentation got him noticed. In 1842, he invented the first fuel cell, which produced electricity by combining hydrogen and oxygen. By showing that steam could be dissociated into oxygen and hydrogen, and the process reversed, he was the first person to demonstrate the thermal dissociation of molecules into their constituent atoms. He built on this work by publishing *On the Correlation of Physical Forces* in 1846, a study that anticipated the theory of the Conservation of Energy. In 1840, he produced an early version of an incandescent light – a predecessor of Edison's electric light patented nearly forty years later. He also collaborated on the development of early photographic processes. He was knighted in 1872 and became a member of the Privy Council in 1887.

Fuel cells are similar to, but not the same as batteries. Batteries have only a limited supply of energy. A fuel cell is continuously supplied with fuel and air. This is why they are used in satellite technology, and in space probes. Stationary fuel cells are used for primary or back-up power in hospitals, offices, schools, hotels and utility plants.

Without fuel cells and ball bearings, our travel, communications and general efficient way of life would be severely impaired.

16

Because a man from Treorchy was a seminal pioneer in the development of the internet and smart cards

Donald Watts Davies was born in Treorchy in 1924. At university in London he gained firsts in physics and mathematics. In the same year, he won the London University Lubbock Memorial Prize as the best mathematician of his year. He proved to be outstanding not only in intellectual power but also in applying his concepts in practice. Working at the National Physical Laboratory, he developed his concept of packet switching. In this sense, a 'packet' is a chunk of data. Packet switching enables computers to talk to each other. He went on as head of a team to build one of the first functioning computer networks. His work was inspirational for the creation of ARPANET, a US defence network being pioneered by Larry Roberts, himself of Welsh descent. ARPANET was the precursor of the internet. So, the work of two Welshmen made the internet a practical proposition.

Davies moved into data security and built systems to protect against malicious interference, especially in financial transactions. He also worked on developing smart cards that provided high-speed encryption and authentication of sender and recipient, allowing EFTPOS (Electronic Funds Transfer at Point of Sale) to be a fundamental element of modern shopping. He was honoured with a CBE in 1983 and made a Fellow of the Royal Society in 1987.

17

Because a Welsh soldier invented lawn tennis

A Welsh Renaissance man, born in Ruabon, Denbighshire, in 1833, Major Walter Clopton Wingfield was a British Army officer, inventor and pioneer of lawn tennis. He secured the patent for the game in February 1874 and had it signed by Queen Victoria. Although this patent ran out in 1877, the game was able to evolve. The earliest versions of modern lawn tennis consisted of a box set that included rubber balls, a net, poles, court markers, and an instruction manual. He envisioned the game being constructed on croquet courts, providing people with healthy exercise and social amusement. His version of the sport spread quickly, and commenced with the first official major championship in 1877 at Wimbledon.

He attended Sandhurst and was commissioned into the 1st Dragoon Guards. Following his retirement from the army in 1870, he was appointed to the Honourable Corps of the Gentlemen at Arms in the court of Queen Victoria.

Wingfield became vice president of the Universal Cookery and Food Association; in 1890, he established Le Cordon Rouge, a society aimed at promoting gourmet standards of food preparation. He styled himself 'Supreme Don' of this movement. He was also active in experimenting with bicycles. In 1997, he was inducted into the International Tennis Hall of Fame. His bust can be found at the Lawn Tennis Museum in Wimbledon.

18

Because mail order and sleeping bags were Welsh inventions in a sleepy town in mid-Wales

Pryce Pryce-Jones was born near Newtown in Montgomeryshire in 1834. In 1856 he took over a drapery business in Newtown specialising in selling Welsh flannel. The railway arrived in 1859, and Pryce-Jones had a bright idea. He pioneered the idea of mail order, selling his Welsh cloth nationally and internationally by parcel post and rail delivery. His 1861 catalogue is said to be the first ever mail-order catalogue. At one time he boasted more than 200,000 customers. In 1861, he patented his Euklisia Rugs, an early style of sleeping bag. As a result he is recognised as the pioneer of the sleeping bag. Pryce-Jones sold 60,000 of them to the Russian Army.

The famed Sears mail order catalogue was published as late as 1892 in the USA. Where would Amazon and camping be if it were not for Pryce-Jones?

Pryce-Jones was elected Conservative MP for Montgomery on 18 December 1885, and he was knighted by Queen Victoria in 1887.

19

Because a gifted Welsh musician preceded Marconi in successful transmission of radio

Wales has pride of place in the development of radio transmissions.

Guglielmo Marconi applied to the Italian Ministry of Post and Telegraphs requesting funding for his pioneering work on telegraphy. He never had the courtesy of a reply. So, aged 21, he came to Britain to further his work.

He erected a 112ft-high transmitting mast on Flat Holm, an island just off Cardiff, and a 98ft receiving mast at Lavernock Point near Penarth. At first, he did not succeed but then in May 1897 he raised his mast to a height of 164ft. This time, his signal in Morse Code, 'Are you ready?' was read clearly. This was the first radio message transmitted over open sea. However, a Welshman from Corwen may deserve the accolade for the first radio transmission eighteen years earlier.

In 1879, David Edward Hughes experimented with a spark transmitter, the signal of which was picked up 500 yards away: he effectively made a radio transmitter and receiver years before Marconi was credited with his transmissions.

Hughes was in fact a musical prodigy and found himself a Professor of Music at St Joseph's College Kentucky at the age of 19. At the age of 20, he was also given the Chair of Philosophy. However, it was as an inventor that he found fame. At the age of 23, he created the teleprinter, whereby a keyboard could produce the corresponding letter on a distant receiver. He returned to Britain and his telegraph invention was adopted as standard. In 1877, he invented the loose-contact carbon microphone – later essential to telephony, sound recording and broadcasting. In 1878, he invented the induction balance, a gizmo still used in metal detectors.

Eight years before Hertz was recognised as identifying radio frequency waves, this Welshman had made the prior discovery. In 1879, he also experimented with powdered copper and electricity and initiated the technology of powder coating. His microphone was the precursor of all carbon microphones currently being used. He received a slew of grand-sounding international awards, including the Order of St Anne from Russia and Commander of the Star and Collar of the Royal Order of Takovo from Serbia. When he died in 1900, most of his assets were bequeathed to four London hospitals.

20

Because the 'father of modern actuarial science' and the first man to make an X-ray tube was Welsh

William Morgan was born in 1750 in Bridgend and proved to be a remarkably gifted man. He worked as an apothecary, physician, physicist and statistician. He wrote two papers on actuarial calculations that won him the Copley Medal in 1789: Morgan is considered to be 'the Father of Modern Actuarial Science'. His experiments in physics led him to submit a paper to the Royal Society in 1785 on phenomena produced by the passage of electricity through a glass tube – the paper was entitled 'Electrical experiments made to ascertain the non-conducting power of a perfect vacuum'. He discovered that when the tube was drained of all air (producing a so-called 'Coolidge vacuum') the electric current could not pass but when he introduced a tiny fraction of air the glass glowed green. Sir Richard Gregory commented on his discovery in 1941, 'Morgan did not know it, but he had produced X-rays and his simple apparatus represented the first X-ray tube.' This line of research was to lead 110 years later to the German physicist Wilhelm Conrad Röntgen naming 'X-rays' as such and taking the first X-ray radiograph of his wife's hand.

21

Because where would modern motoring be without the Welsh inventions of spare tyres and tarmac?

Stepney Street in Llanelli derives its name from the seventeenth-century line of Stepney family baronets who settled in the area. They in turn had their origins in the Stepney area of London.

In 1906, brothers Walter and Tom Davies registered the Stepney Spare Motor Wheel as a company in Llanelli. They had begun an ironmongery business there in Stepney Street in 1895, and had the bright idea of producing spare wheels for cars. At that time vehicles were sold without a spare and since roads at this time were liberally littered with horseshoe nails, flat tyres were a common problem. Their invention consisted of an inflated tyre on a circular rim that could be simply clamped over a flat tyre to cure the problem.

The Davies brothers found themselves supplying a worldwide demand. Their 1909 catalogue boasted that their Stepney tyres were fitted to all London taxis. The Davies brothers made a lot of money until, in the wake of the end of the First World War, car manufacturers incorporated a spare wheel as standard.

The name lives on with linguistic reverberations. Spare wheels are still called Stepneys in the former British colonies of India, Bangladesh and Malta. By extension, mistresses (spare wives) are also often called Stepneys in India.

In 1783, John McAdam pioneered a new road surfacing technique involving crushed stone. This was an improvement for horses and horse-drawn vehicles but macadam, as it came to be known, was not adequate for the age of the motor car. The stones would slip, the macadam would suffer rutting, and the jagged edges of the stone caused innumerable flat tyres. A county surveyor, Edgar Purnell Hooley, hailing from Swansea, noticed a particularly smooth surface near an ironworks in Denby. He found out that a barrel of tar had spilled onto the road and someone had poured waste slag onto the surface to cover up the mess. The result was a solid road surface without rutting, dust or pesky sharp stones. In 1902, he applied for a patent for his invention of tarmacadam. Tarmacadam or Tarmac was a big improvement on macadam alone as a road surface. Tarmac added tar and sand to the macadam and was a much more durable product. Hooley went on to found the company Tar Macadam Syndicate Ltd, later to become Tarmac Ltd, one of the largest building supply companies in Britain.

22

Because two Welsh actors have exported their talent to become internationally acclaimed stars

Damian Watcyn Lewis was born in London in 1971. As his middle name suggests, his paternal grandparents were Welsh. He was to become a globally recognised actor. He portrayed Bobby Axelrod in the Showtime drama *Billions* for the first time in 2016, a series that was to run for five seasons. His first real break came playing Major Richard D. Winters in the HBO miniseries *Band of Brothers* (2001). He followed this up with the role of sociopath Soames Forsyte in *The Forsyte Saga* (2002–03). His performance as Gunnery Sergeant Nicholas Brody in the Showtime series *Homeland* won him a Golden Globe Award and Primetime Emmy Award. In 2015, he played the Tudor King Henry VIII in the dramatisation of *Wolf Hall*. He won a CBE in the Birthday Honours in 2022 for services to drama and charity. In interviews he has said, 'I'm proud of my Welsh roots,' 'I love coming to Wales' and 'I will always say I'm British, not English.'

Lewis played alongside Ioan Gruffudd in *Warriors*, a BBC TV drama from 1999 featuring the dilemmas and difficulties of British soldiers acting as peacekeepers in Bosnia. Gruffudd also featured in *The Forsyte Saga* as Bosinney, the architect who builds a country house for Soames and has an affair with Soames's wife, Irene. Gruffudd has described himself as 'very fervently Welsh'. He was born in Aberdare in 1973.

In 2000, *Solomon & Gaenor* was nominated in the Oscars for Best Foreign Language Film. The film is a gritty romance between a Jewish lad and a Welsh girl during an anti-Semitic period in the Welsh valleys. It was produced by the Welsh language channel S4C and filmed back to back in English and Welsh; it was the Welsh version that was nominated. The lead actors were both Welsh: Ioan Gruffudd and Nia Roberts. Gruffudd is a Welsh institution in himself, having starred, *inter alia*, in the TV series *Hornblower*, *Poldark* and the films *Titanic*, *Black Hawk Down* and *King Arthur*.

Gruffudd also starred in the ABC crime drama series *Forever* in 2014–15. It ran for twenty-two episodes, attracting audiences in the millions. Its central character was Dr Henry Morgan, who is a medical examiner who is also trying to solve the riddle of his own immortality. Afterwards, in 2018–21 he played a forensic pathologist in the hit Australian series *Harrow*, which ran for three series over thirty episodes. Gruffudd's first language is Welsh and in 2003 he was inducted into the Bardic Order of Great Britain at Meifod.

As in other fields, the best actors, writers, directors and creative artists tend to be exported worldwide rather than ascend a career ladder in Wales. Gruffudd lives in Los Angeles, while Lewis also lived in LA for some time but currently lives in London, although he also has a property in Carmarthenshire.

23

Because one of the greatest box-office stars of the twentieth century was born in humble beginnings in Wales

Richard Jenkins was born on 10 November 1925 in Pontrhydyfen, Glamorgan. Richard was the twelfth of thirteen children born into a Welsh-speaking family. His was a humble background and he had a difficult start. His father was a miner, who was prone to drinking binges (Richard took after his father in this respect). His mother died when he was aged 2. He eventually came under the wing of a schoolmaster, Philip Burton, who became his surrogate father and nurtured his talents and became his legal guardian. Richard had his surname changed by deed poll to Burton.

As an actor, Richard Burton ascended into the ranks of the top box office stars. He began his career in 1943 but made his name on the West End Stage in the 1950s and was talked of as an heir to Olivier. His stage presence and rich, sonorous voice were renowned. He starred in fifty-five films including *Cleopatra*, *The Longest Day*, *The Spy Who Came in From the Cold*, *Becket*, *Equus*, *The Night of the Iguana* and *Anne of the Thousand Days*. By the late 1960s, he was one of the highest-paid actors in the world, receiving fees of more than $1 million. He told a chat show host in 2014, 'I am tremendously proud of being Welsh.' He commented also on his rich voice, 'It's a deep, dark answer from the Valleys to everything.' He was awarded a CBE in 1970.

Burton married five times, most notably twice to Elizabeth Taylor. He was friends with Marshal Tito, then President of Yugoslavia, whom he met before playing him in the film *The Battle of Sutjeska*. Burton was also a great raconteur and mimic, and it is little known that he was a fluent Welsh speaker. He should have been knighted. He died at the age of 58 in 1984. A book of Dylan Thomas's poems is buried with him.

24

Because a Welsh actor was recognised by the film industry as one of both the greatest villains and sexiest stars

In 1992, Alan Rickman won the Evening Standard Drama Award for Best Actor for his film performances. During his career he won seven awards in all. His mother, Margaret, came from Treforest, near Pontypridd. His first feature film involved playing the villain, Hans Gruber, in *Die Hard* in 1988. His languid, sneering voice made him a good choice for the role of 'baddy'. He played the Sheriff of Nottingham in *Robin Hood: Prince of Thieves* (1991) and Severus Snape, the enigmatic potions master, in the Harry Potter film franchise. He is the only actor who made it on to the Greatest Villains List twice. He is memorialised underneath the 'Platform 9¾' sign at London's King's Cross railway station. He was recognised by the American Film Industry as being one of the best villains in cinema history. This may well be connected with his unique voice, which could convey sneer and menace.

In counterpoint, Rickman's voice could also communicate depth and romance, and he did not want to be typecast as a villain. He starred as romantic leads in films such as *Truly, Madly, Deeply* (1991) and in the rom-com *Love Actually* (2003) as Harry, a wayward husband. *Love*

Actually won the Empire Award as Best Film and grossed £247 million at the box office. He was chosen by *Empire* magazine as one of the 100 Sexiest Stars in film history in 1995.

Although his accent was RP English, Rickman felt himself very much a Celt and was always proud of his Celtic roots. 'There's not a lot of English blood in me,' he once said. *The Independent* once quoted him as saying, 'It's a huge thing when you have Celtic blood running in your veins, and not English; there's an inherited energy.'

25

Because the most beautiful woman on the planet, named after a cargo ship, rose to stardom playing alongside a cockney wide boy with Welsh roots

The Welsh beauty Catherine Zeta-Jones was born in Swansea in September 1969. She was Catherine Jones at birth and acquired the Zeta to mark her out from a sea of other Welsh Joneses. *Zeta* was a cargo ship (gross tonnage 8,742 tons) sailing out of Swansea. Catherine was a precocious performer, becoming British Tap-Dancing Champion at the age of 13. Her dancing lessons were financed by a lucky bingo win by her parents. Her triumphs include *The Mask of Zorro* in 1998 (grossing $250 million worldwide) and as Virginia Baker co-starring with Sean Connery in *Entrapment* in 1999 (it grossed $212 million at the box office). She has starred in a variety of films including *The Haunting* (1999, grossing $180 million) and *Chicago* (2002, this time grossing $307 million). She was awarded a CBE for her film and charity work in 2010. She has also won a Tony Award, an Academy Award and two Golden Globes. She has two children by the actor Michael Douglas. In her own words, 'I drink, I swear, I like sex.' *Esquire* magazine once described her as the most beautiful woman on the planet.

Zeta-Jones's first big break was acting the part of Mariette in the TV series *The Darling Buds of May*. She starred alongside David Jason, whose mother, Olwen, was Welsh. He lived for eighteen years in Taff's Well with his long-term partner, Myfanwy Talog. In 2005, there was a poll to identify British TV's greatest stars. Jason took first place. He was knighted that year for his services to acting and comedy. He has won four British Academy Television Awards (BAFTAs), four British Comedy Awards and seven National Television Awards. He has also written three autobiographies. Lovely jubbly!

26

Because two talented Welsh knights both played popes in a film with 'outstanding performances from its well-matched leads'[1]

John Price was born in Carmel, Flintshire, in 1947. Better known as the actor Jonathan Pryce, he has won two Olivier Awards and two Tonys. Notably, he played Thomas Wolsey in the BBC series *Wolf Hall* and the sinister High Sparrow in HBO's series *Game of Thrones*. He was knighted in the Birthday Honours 2021 for services to drama and charity. He once told *The Guardian*, 'I'd rather be Welsh than English, that's for sure.' He also played Prince Philip in the fifth series of *The Crown*, released in 2022.

The popular Netflix film *The Two Popes* was released in November 2019. Both the popes were played by Welshmen. Pryce portrayed Pope Francis and Anthony Hopkins played Pope Benedict XVI. Interestingly, in 2020 they were both nominated for Oscars for their performances in this film.

1991 saw the release of the film *The Silence of the Lambs*, which was destined to gross an impressive $273 million at the box office. Hopkins played the villain of the piece, the cannibal Hannibal Lecter. Hopkins

---

[1] According to the review aggregator Rotten Tomatoes.

was born in Port Talbot in 1937. He studied acting at Cardiff's College of Music and Drama. He has starred in many films, including taking the title role in *Nixon*; he also played the American-Welsh President John Quincy Adams in *Amistad*. The late film producer Lord Attenborough described Hopkins as 'unquestionably the greatest actor of his generation' after he had acted in his two films, *Young Winston* and *A Bridge Too Far*. He won an Oscar for *The Silence of the Lambs*; three BAFTA awards for the same film and two others; and two Emmys for being the Outstanding Lead Actor in a Limited Series or TV Programme (for *The Lindbergh Kidnapping Case* and *The Bunker*). He was knighted by Queen Elizabeth II in 1993. He won a star on the Hollywood Walk of Fame in 2003.

27

Because Wales produced a great free thinker, defender of free speech and Nobel Prize winner

Bertrand Russell was born and died in Wales (1872–1970). He gained firsts in mathematics and moral sciences from Trinity College, Cambridge. He quickly became a philosopher of world renown. His early work, *Principia Mathematica* (three volumes published between 1910 and 1913) moved British philosophy in a more scientific direction. In 1928, he wrote, 'The fundamental argument for freedom of opinion is the doubtfulness of all our belief ... when the State intervenes to ensure the indoctrination of some doctrine, it does so because there is no conclusive evidence in favour of that doctrine.' His socialist leanings would not have made him sympathetic to cancel culture or the government's Counter-Disinformation Unit: 'It is clear that thought is not free if the profession of certain opinions make it impossible to make a living.' (*Skeptical Essays*, 1929) He was notably sceptical about the official version of who killed J.F. Kennedy.

Russell wrote ninety books, of which *The History of Western Philosophy* (1946) stands out in particular. Despite his anti-establishment, pacifist attitudes and his being jailed for an anti-nuclear protest, King George VI awarded him the Order of Merit on 9 June 1949, with the following words, 'You have sometimes behaved in a manner that would not do if generally adopted.' Russell just smiled but said that this reply came to mind, 'Yes, that's right, just like your brother.'

In 1950, he was awarded a Nobel Prize in Literature 'in recognition of his varied and significant writings in which he champions humanitarian ideals and freedom of thought'.

In 1953, he argued that '[where there is dictatorship] diet, injections, and injunctions will combine, from a very early age, to produce the sort of character and the sort of beliefs that the authorities consider desirable, and any serious criticism of the powers that be will become psychologically impossible. Even if all are miserable, all will believe themselves happy, because the government will tell them that they are so.'

28

Because south Wales was a hotbed of Chartism that eventually shaped much of our modern democracy

In 1839, there was a Chartist meeting at the Coach and Horses public house (now demolished) in Blackwood where they took a decision to hold a large demonstration in Newport. The Chartist lodges in the district all held meetings on 2 November and pledged to join a revolt, seize Newport and stop the Mail. The march turned violent on 4 November and twenty-two demonstrators were killed. The violent side of the Chartist movement was discredited. The aims of Chartism were:

All men to have the vote (universal manhood suffrage)
Voting should take place by secret ballot
Members of Parliament should be paid
The property qualification for becoming a Member of Parliament should be abolished
Constituencies should be of equal size
Parliamentary elections every year, not once every five years

The first four aims were eventually fully achieved. The fifth is not fully achieved but Boundary Commissions are established periodically to recommend roughly fair allotments of constituency by size. The sixth has been ruled out by the wisdom of Brenda from Bristol.

29

Because a Welsh-speaking democracy set up 7,000 miles away from Wales was the first to enfranchise women

In July 1865, 150 settlers from Wales arrived by ship from Liverpool at Puerto Madryn in Argentina, having travelled 7,000 miles hoping to establish Y Wladfa (a Welsh-speaking colony in Patagonia). At a time when the Welsh language was forbidden in Welsh schools, the settlers wanted to escape anglicisation. The settlers had the aim of preserving the Welsh way of life and the Welsh language. The Argentines had offered 100 square miles of land along the Chubut River. Unfortunately, the settlers found that Patagonia was not the fertile land they had envisaged. Life at first was hard on this windswept pampas and the Tehuelche Indians helped them through their initial difficulties – as did the establishment of an irrigation system stemming from the River Chubut that turned large tracts of unproductive terrain into viable farm land – and more settlers arrived from both Wales and Pennsylvania.

By 1874, the settlement had a population of 270, with a pattern of farms beginning to emerge. In 1875, the Welsh settlers were granted official title to the land by Argentina, and this encouraged new settlers to join the colony, with more than 500 arriving from Wales. The settlers had achieved their goal with Welsh-speaking chapels, schools and local government. However, over time the culture has blended and diluted with Spanish. There are said to be 50,000 people in Patagonia of Welsh descent and some 5,000 who speak Welsh. They can communicate very well with Welsh speakers from Wales, except that the Patagonian Welsh speakers speak the language with a Spanish accent and say 'thankyiw' for thank you, whereas the Welsh say 'diolch'.

For the first ten years the Welsh settlement was self-governing with its constitution written in Welsh. Women had a right to vote – indeed it seems this was the first democracy in the world to enfranchise women. Nowadays, eisteddfods are still held in the towns of Gaiman, Trefelin and Trelew. There are three bilingual Welsh–Spanish primary schools and each year about 1,000 people are learning to speak Welsh there. Y Wladfa has an anthem derived from the Welsh National Anthem.

30

Because one of Clint Eastwood's favourite films is based on a novel about a Welsh mining community

Richard Dafydd Vivian Llewellyn Lloyd was born in 1906, and with a name like that it is no surprise that he was born to Welsh parents. He was later to become famous as a writer under the nom de plume Richard Llewellyn. His best-known novel was *How Green Was My Valley* (published in 1939). *The New York Times* described it as, 'The most magnificent novel ever produced about Wales,' and it went on to earn the 1940 National Book Award. The on-screen adaptation was filmed by John Ford in 1941, and was nominated for ten Academy Awards, including Outstanding Motion Picture. It won five Academy Awards, beat *Citizen Kane* to Best Picture and is still screened regularly on British television.

Few will forget the final scenes from the film when the distraught lad, Huw Morgan, played by Roddy McDowall, searches for his father, Gwilym, in the collapsed and flooded pit. 'Da-da!' Huw cries repeatedly, and it echoes hauntingly around the mine. Huw finds him buried beneath a pit prop, but nothing can be done and Gwilym passes away. Huw later narrates, 'Men like my father cannot die. They are with me still, real in memory as they were in flesh, loving and beloved forever.'

Llewellyn's best-selling novel was followed by *Up Into the Singing Mountain* (1960), *And I Shall Sleep ... Down Where the Moon is*

Small (1966), and *Green, Green My Valley Now* (1975). Llewellyn was a captain in the Welsh Guards during the Second World War. He wrote two successful mystery plays and various other novels. He always claimed to be Welsh, but some critics have been sniffy about it because he was brought up in Hendon, but in an era of self-definition that criticism seems overblown. Criticism might more fairly be directed at the film of *How Green Was My Valley* in that it was filmed not in Wales but California, and that it was almost entirely devoid of Welsh actors. Pastiche it may have been, but some pastiche can embed deep into a national psyche.

31

Because a Welsh transgender pioneer won an award for her lifetime's services to literature

Jan Morris, born in 1926 to a Welsh engineer, served in the Second World War in the 9th Queen's Royal Lancers. As a correspondent for *The Times*, Morris accompanied the Hillary expedition on its successful conquest of Everest in 1953, on which she was the only journalist. In 1949, she married Elizabeth and they had five children together. In 1972, she received gender-affirming surgery to transition to a woman – one of the first high-profile people to do so. She had to travel to Morocco to receive the procedure. Morris was later to write an autobiography about her transition, *Conundrum* (1974). She was well known for her travel writing and was hailed as the 'Flaubert of the Jet Age'. Morris also specialised in history. Her trilogy *Pax Britannica* won praise as a positive analysis of the British Empire, although she was a passionate Welsh nationalist and republican. Her biography of Admiral Jackie Fisher, *Fisher's Face* (1985), is an intriguing character analysis. Although Fisher modernised the Royal Navy in preparation for the First World War, during that war he seems to have experienced a mental breakdown. Morris was elected as a druid in 1992. In 1999, she received a CBE in the Queen's Birthday Honours. She wrote fifty-eight books in all. In 2005, she received the Golden Pen Award from English PEN for her 'Lifetime's Distinguished Service to Literature'.

32

Because one of the most prolific, popular and raunchy authors of TV and cinema is a Cardiff boy

Andrew Wynford Davies was born in Rhiwbina, Cardiff, in September 1936, son of Wynford Davies, who – remarkably – was the French teacher of one of the authors at Cardiff High School for Boys and also of our father. Andrew Davies said in 2014, 'I had a very high opinion of my father's judgement of things and he said, "You better get a job that pays the bills because a writer doesn't make any money."' It is just as well for all of us that in this instance he ignored his father's advice.

Davies began his career as a teacher like his father, but a teacher of English. Nevertheless, his destiny was to write. He developed into a playwright, script writer and novelist of global renown. He has written forty-three TV series and dramas and thirty-nine television plays. His cinema script writing features, among others, *The Tailor of Panama*, *Brideshead Revisited* (2008) and two Bridget Jones films. Among his many television series, *To Serve Them All My Days* (1980), *A Very Peculiar Practice* (1986–88), *Pride and Prejudice* (featuring a dripping wet Colin Firth in 1995), *Tipping the Velvet* (2002), *Mr Selfridge* (2013–14), *Les Misérables* (2019), *Sanditon* (2019) and *A Suitable Boy* (2020) stand out. His TV adaptation of Michel Dobbs's *House of Cards* was first screened in 1990. Davies claims authorship of the line, 'You might very well think that; I couldn't possibly comment.' Both he and Dobbs were accredited executive producers for the American series. His BBC film, *A Poet in New York* (2014) tells the story of the last days of Dylan Thomas in that city. *The Daily Telegraph* commented that his 'script came from one of the few writers who could hope to do the poet justice'.

His father – the French teacher – once told a class of incredulous adolescent boys at Cardiff High School that sex wasn't everything – friendship was key to a relationship. Davies recognises that he may have gone beyond his father's strait-laced advice. 'I don't think everything I have written since has been to his taste!' He has a reputation for infidelity to the original in his adaptations and for sexing up the scenes. It sells well to modern audiences.

In 2014, he said: 'I'd quite like to go back ... to write about my parents and my own life as a kid and all the stuff that I couldn't write about directly, or felt I couldn't when my parents were alive.' Ah, hiraeth. We hope he fulfils that ambition.

33

Because a pilot, spy, oilman, novelist and inventor born in Cardiff became one of the greatest storytellers for children of the twentieth century

Roald Dahl was born in 1916 in Cardiff. He was very much influenced by his early life in Cardiff as he described in his 1984 autobiography *Boy: Tales of Childhood*. He wrote fondly about his early life there, although there was a hiccup when he was caned at school for having put a dead mouse into a jar of gobstoppers in the sweetshop in Llandaff owned by a very unpleasant and sour-looking Mrs Pratchett. The building is no longer a sweet shop but sports a blue plaque in Dahl's honour. He had a kaleidoscopic career as air force pilot, spy, oilman, novelist, poet, chocolate historian and medical inventor (he invented a one-way valve to drain the brain of his son, Theo, who had become hydrocephalic after a car accident in 1960). But, it is as a writer of tales for children that he is most famous: *Matilda, George's Marvellous Medicine, James and the Giant Peach, The Witches, The BFG, The Enormous Crocodile, Charlie and the Great Glass Elevator, The Twits, Charlie and the Chocolate Factory* and *Fantastic Mr Fox* are just some of the magical books that tumbled out of his prolific pen. As he wrote sagely in one of these books, 'A little nonsense now and then is relished by the wisest men.' Among the awards heaped upon him were the British Books Awards' Children's Author of the Year in 1990 and the World Fantasy Award for Lifetime Achievement in 1983. There is a public piazza in Cardiff Bay named after him, Roald Dahl Plass.

34

Because Wales was at the leading edge of aviation technology

The Wright brothers were not the first pioneers of flight. It was a Welshman on 24 September 1896. The Wrights first flew in 1903 and then only for 30 yards. Bill Frost, a simple carpenter from Saundersfoot, patented his flying machine in 1894 (European Patent Office GB189420431). He then proceeded to build it. Its lift was provided by a hydrogen-filled balloon assisted by two vertical take-off horizontal fans. When the plane was aloft the wings tilted forward and allowed the structure to glide. The structure was 31ft long and was constructed of wire mesh, canvas and bamboo. Steering was by means of a rudder. The day Frost chose to fly in 1896 there was a gale, and although he managed to stay airborne for between 500 and 600 yards his plane clipped the top of a tree in Saundersfoot, and it was brought down in a field. Frost never found the backing or resources to rebuild and relaunch. The far-seeing War Department dismissed his application for support, claiming that, 'The nation does not intend to adopt aerial navigation as a means of warfare'. Bill Frost died in 1935 but *The Sunday Times* acknowledged on 26 July 1998 that this 'Welsh airman beat the Wrights to the skies'.

In the first decade of the twentieth century, Cardiff was the airship centre of the world, and the acknowledged 'Father of British Airships' was a Cardiff man in his twenties, E.T. Willows. He was training to follow his father as a dentist, but the profession was not for him. Despite his lack of engineering training, he built his first airship, *Willows I*, in a hangar in Splott. He flew it for the first time in August 1905 and stayed aloft for eighty-five minutes. Colonel Capper from the War Office later claimed that the government's own airship, *Nulli Secundus*, built in 1907, was 'a very bad second to the Willows I'.

Willows later boldly experimented with *Willows II* around the skies of Cardiff in 1910. This airship was double the size of *Willows I*, being 86ft long and carrying 21,000ft^3 of gas. *Willows II* had swivel propellers, which made use of the principle of dynamic lift in a revolutionary way. Using these propellers, Willows could make his airship rise or fall at a slope of 1 in 7. It could climb at a rate of 1,000ft a minute.

Willows undertook an historic flight from Cardiff to London in August 1910 – it was the furthest flight yet in a dirigible. He flew at night – no doubt it was easier to navigate the craft in the cool night air. His father entered into the spirit of the adventure by trying to guide him by the lights of his car beneath, until the vehicle broke down. Willows pressed on and attempted to get his bearings by the glittering lights of the towns beneath. In all, he had to drop close to the ground a dozen times, and hail the startled folk below using a megaphone to ask them directions to London. They must have been quite taken aback by this new technology lumbering out of the darkness at them, rather like a science fiction close encounter.

Willows ran out of fuel, but drifted over Crystal Palace, and eventually managed to land at Lee, near Mottingham. Willows had accomplished a record for cross-country flight in Britain: impressive for a lad of 24. On his arrival, Willows gave an interview to the *Cardiff Times*, saying, 'I prefer airships to aeroplanes because you can economise on fuel and stay up longer. We must overcome the diffusion of gas – its percolation through the envelope – and then we can stay up for three days together. By getting to higher altitudes we can rise above bad winds and foul weather.'

Willows next set himself the goal of a nonstop flight from London to Paris in his biggest airship yet, *Willows III*. It was 120ft long, carried 32,000ft^3 of gas and could rise 6,500ft in twelve minutes. Renamed the *City of Cardiff*, the airship took off for France from Wormwood Scrubs on 4 November 1910 at 3.25 p.m. watched by Asquith (then prime minister), Churchill and Lloyd George. Willows ran into thick fog at 3,000ft. The charts were dropped by mistake, so he had little knowledge of his bearings. The engine had to stop more than once because of mechanical defects, and eventually a slack envelope forced him down nose first near Douai. This had been the first Channel crossing by airship at night.

The airship was not too badly damaged, but bureaucracy loomed in the form of surly French customs officials demanding £30 for the

Willows II, a record-breaking dirigible.

import duty on the gas in the airship. Urgent representations by the Aero Club of France resulted in Willows being given a month to leave or pay up. After several more mishaps and adverse weather (sometimes causing his petrol to freeze in the carburettor), Willows finally made it to Paris on 28 December. On New Year's Eve, he triumphantly circled the Eiffel Tower. Willows left France before customs could stick him with the duty.

On his return to Britain, Willows began work on *Willows IV*. This airship was smaller and more streamlined than *Willows III*, with a length of 110ft and a capacity of 20,000ft^3. It was bought by the Navy for £1,050 and in 1912 *Willows IV* became His Majesty's Naval Airship No. 2. On its first test it reached the impressive speed of 50mph.

Willows began construction of his most ambitious airship yet, *Willows V*. It was 130ft long and had a capacity of 50,000ft^3 – four times as big as *Willows I*. It could carry four people and travel at up to 38mph. In February 1914, *Willows V* flew over central London, circling St Paul's and paying respects to the Houses of Parliament and Buckingham Palace. The final fate of *Willows V* is a mystery.

In 1917, Willows was called in to advise the services on kite balloons (similar to barrage balloons of the Second World War). He made significant improvements in a matter of days and enormously strengthened British defences against German air raids.

In the last years of the war Willows manufactured kite balloons in Cardiff. The government contracted for eighty-three balloons, and at the height Willows employed as many as 150 staff. However, the Armistice led to the winding down of the business. Although his firm resolve was to make Cardiff 'one of the foremost ports of the air', his ambitions died with him in a ballooning accident in 1926.

35

Because a Welshman overthrew the House of York, won the crown of England, ended the Wars of the Roses and founded a new dynamic dynasty – the Tudors

Henry Tudor was born at Pembroke Castle in 1457. His grandfather, Owain, had impregnated Catherine, widow of the Welsh king, Henry V, although his main claim to the English throne was through his mother, Margaret Beaufort. While in exile in France, he gathered together some 2,000 men (Welsh, French and Scots) and set sail for Milford Haven, where he landed in August 1485. He marched through Wales, picking up more supporters on his way to challenge Richard III to battle at Bosworth. On his way, Henry consulted a Welsh bard and seer at Mathafarn in Powys on 11 August 1485. The poet, Dafydd Llwyd, gave him his prophecy in the form of a poem in Welsh (which we suspect indicates that Henry did speak Welsh). A modern English translation shows that Dafydd predicted the downfall of the 'caterpillar' (the 'crookback' Richard). Henry, with 4,500 troops, was facing a potential army of 13,500 Yorkists, so the prophecy was against the odds. Although he was outnumbered, Henry won the battle decisively.

When he was crowned Henry VII on 30 October 1485, it was said that he fulfilled a prophecy: Edward II's biographer wrote of the Welsh that, 'According to the sayings of the Welsh prophet Merlin they will one day repossess England.' The historian Trevelyan was later to write, 'On a bare Leicestershire upland a few thousand men in close conflict foot to foot ... sufficed to set upon the throne of England the greatest of all her royal lines, that should guide her through a century of change down new and larger streams of history.' Trevisan, a Venetian writer, reported, 'The Welsh may now be said to have recovered their former independence, for the most wise and fortunate Henry VII is a Welshman.' Francis Bacon wrote, 'To the Welsh people, his victory was theirs; they had thereby regained their independence.'

Henry VII punctiliously observed St David's Day after ascending the throne, and educated his elder son, Arthur, to speak Welsh. He established the Tudor dynasty with peace and stability, ending the Wars of the Roses. With typical Welsh attention to thrift, he left the royal finances on a healthy basis when he died. He was buried at Westminster Abbey in 1509.

36

Because of the man who made Welsh nationalism respectable

Gwynfor Evans was born in Barry in 1912 and became fluent in Welsh by the age of 17. On 14 July 1966, he became the first Plaid Cymru (Welsh Nationalist) MP elected to Parliament in a by-election in Carmarthen after the death of Lady Megan Lloyd George, who had been the incumbent Labour MP in the seat. This was a sensational breakthrough for Plaid Cymru. *The Scotsman* newspaper called him, 'The man who made Plaid Cymru credible.'

He was not just a trailblazer for nationalism in Wales. He tried to take the Oath of Allegiance in the Commons in Welsh but was refused, but this right was granted during his lifetime in 1974. He was a constant campaigner for better road links to west Wales, earning him the nickname of 'Evans Dual Carriageway'; again, in his lifetime he saw the final completion of the M4 corridor in Wales in 1993 – an artery that has been a magnet for economic development in south Wales along its length. He was a fervent proponent of a Welsh Parliament: again in his lifetime, in 1999 the National Assembly for Wales was set up as a devolved administration. It now calls itself the Welsh Parliament. He also pushed tirelessly for a separate Welsh language TV channel. This was achieved in 1980 as S4C. The threat of Gwynfor going on hunger strike made the then Conservative government concede to his aim. Sadly, S4C subsequently lost its independence to the BBC. Gwynfor passed away in 2005.

37

Because Sarah Jane Rees of Llangranog was a woman ahead of her time – master mariner, editor, international preacher, first woman to gain a Bardic Crown and an acknowledged inspiration

Sarah Jane Rees was born into a respectable and relatively comfortable family in 1839 in the small fishing village of Llangrannog, Ceredigion. Her father was a master mariner. This part of rural west Wales was dominated by agriculture, shipping and fishing. Cardigan was several days' journey from the fledgling industrial areas of south Wales before the advent of the train. As a port, Cardigan was losing its prominence on the west Wales coast, taking pioneers to their new lives in Canada and engaging in international trade with America. However, small trading ships, sloops, ketches and smacks would ply their trade of coal and other cargo up and down the coast to ports along the Welsh coast and Ireland. The aspiration of most young men would be to become a master mariner and captain ships. This was where money could be made but where the dangers were great. The aspirations of most middle-class women would be to marry well. The authors' grandmother was born into a similar family in the late nineteenth century with the same expectations. Being strong minded, she was able to break with convention, and with the advent of the First World War pursued a career in nursing and qualified in 1919 at the age of 29.

From an early age Rees had an interest in following her father into his trade but after finishing at the local school at 13 she was sent to Cardigan to learn dressmaking. This was not a success. She returned home, joined her father on his ketch and travelled around the coast of Wales, France, Liverpool and Ireland with cargo. Having qualified as a master mariner in London, she returned to her village to teach at the local school, where her lessons included aspects of seafaring. Later, she taught navigation at the John Evans School in Aberystwyth. She had also developed a passion for writing poetry.

In 1865 Rees entered the National Eisteddfod at Aberystwyth with her poem and became the first woman to win the bardic crown. All entries were anonymous and Cranogwen was her bardic name. Her winning poem, 'Y Fodrwy Briodasol', a moving account of a married woman's lot, beat the leading bards of the day, Islwyn and Ceiriog. She had further successes at Chester the following year and won in Caerphilly and Aberaeron in 1873 with her long poem in free verse on the wreck of the north fleet, 'Drylliad y north fleet'.

Rees published a book of poetry in 1870, *Caniadau Cranogwen*. She wrote on a broad range of themes, such as nature, her love of Wales, her Christian faith, the evils of drink, storms and shipwrecks, and was very popular. She decided to leave teaching and followed her vocation of preaching and lecturing. She was deeply religious and was an expressive and eloquent speaker, travelling in Wales and through Welsh communities in America. She received some opposition to her prominent position as a woman preaching but was supported by Thomas Levi, a prominent non-conformist leader. The British newspapers of this time reported her tours widely both in Wales and England.

Her trailblazing continued with her editing a Welsh-language women's magazine, *Y Frythones* – once again, the first Welsh woman in such a position. It was aimed primarily at working-class young women and included stories and poems, providing a platform for women writers. The publication encouraged secondary and higher education for women as well as advocating opportunities for women to earn independent and respectable livings.

Rees continued her preaching and aimed to improve the moral welfare in industrialised south Wales. Owing to her religious beliefs, the temperance movement was very important to her. She founded Undeb Dirwestol Merched y De, the South Wales Women's Temperance Union. There were 140 branches throughout south Wales at the time of her death.

Cranogwen died at the home of her niece in Cilfynydd, Pontypridd, on 27 June 1916, and was buried in the churchyard of St Carannog's Church, Llangrannog. Once again, both Welsh and English newspapers reported her death with glowing obituaries and details of memorial services.

Cranogwen broke down intellectual, cultural, professional and personal barriers. She never married but had two long-term partners, Fanny Rees, who died in 1874, and Jane Thomas, who remained her partner until her death.

In pondering the achievements of such an extraordinary life some two hundred years ago, we were puzzled by the lack of knowledge of this formidable groundbreaker within the wider community until recently. Was this due to the patriarchy of history? However, this was a woman who deeply affected both men and women with her drive and inspiration on behalf of the people of Wales.

In 2016 a small not-for-profit organisation, Monumental Welsh Women, was created to celebrate the achievements of remarkable Welsh women, none of whom had ever been commemorated by a statue. In June 2023, the third statue of five was unveiled and erected in the birthplace of this prodigious woman who achieved so much in a world dominated by patriarchy and where there were limited opportunities for women of any birth status.

On 3 January 1936, an article appeared in the *Western Mail* by Grace Roberts, politician and journalist and one of the first women in Wales to stand as MP – the other being Megan Lloyd George. Roberts confessed that she had never been privileged to meet Cranogwen but she knew of illustrious Welshmen who claimed their success rested on her inspiration. In the opinion of the Parliamentarian Sir Ellis Griffith, 'If Cranogwen had been a Member of Parliament ... she would have advocated the needs of Wales more effectively than all the members of the Welsh Parliamentary Party put together.'

In 1939, the *Merthyr Express* posted details of her centenary celebration. After nearly twenty-five years Cranogwen was still an acclaimed poet. Sporadic newspaper entries commemorating her life appear until the mid-1950s and then peter out. We hope there will be great celebrations in 2039 to commemorate her bicentenary and life and work.

Professor Deirdre Beddoe, Emeritus Professor of Women's History at the University of Glamorgan, had this to say of her: she was 'a tall, dark, striking woman, strong-willed and supremely confident, but possessed of a delightful sense of humour. Cranogwen was, without doubt, the most outstanding Welsh woman of the nineteenth century.'

38

Because a one-legged Welsh tramp living in a doss house wrote some of the most popular poetry of his day

In 1871, a man who was to make his reputation as a transatlantic tramp was born in Wales. William Henry Davies was born in Newport, Monmouthshire, in humble circumstances. Leaving his apprenticeship as a picture framer, he travelled to the United States, where he became a drifter, doing occasional work, but also finding his way to pass the winter in Michigan exploiting the so-called boodle system by paying to while away his time in a variety of prisons. He recorded his experiences of wandering around the US between 1893 and 1899 in his smash hit book *Autobiography of a Supertramp*, published in 1908. It is still in print today. He decided to try to make his fortune by hitching a ride on a train to join the Klondike Gold Rush in 1899 but he fell off and his foot was run over by the wheel of the train, resulting in his lower right leg being amputated. Gold prospecting was not to be. He returned to Britain, and lived rough or in hostels.

Davies was eventually to move from doss house to distinction. He turned the rest of his life to poetry and became the best-known poet of his age, publishing some twenty collections. One of his poems, 'Leisure', presages the modern prescription of mindfulness:

What is this life if, full of care,
We have no time to stand and stare.

Davies died in his comfortable detached home in Nailsea on 26 September 1940.

39

Because a fifteenth-century Welsh poet was 500 years ahead of English-speaking writers in celebrating the wonder of female genitals

There is sometimes a tendency to describe the Welsh as being somewhat strait-laced in sexual matters. This is connected, no doubt, to waves of attempted suppression by religious movements. However, beneath the veneer there lies a different story.

Gwerful Mechain was a female poet who lived in about 1460–1502. She came from Mechain, Powys in Mid-Wales. Katie Gramich's anthology of her work published in 2018 contains Gwerful's poems in their original Welsh, together with English translations. Remarkably, Gwerful's erotic writing in the Middle Ages was some 500 years ahead of her time in her forthright celebration of the charms of the female genitals. Not until 1996 was *The Vagina Monologues* produced, encouraging women to empower themselves through open discussion of their genitals. Gwerful's poetry is frank and to the point in her poem 'Cywydd y Cedor' (Verse of the Vulva), which accuses her lover of effectively ignoring the best bit.

The erotic poet, Dafydd ap Gwilym (*c.*1315–50) pre-dated Gwerful Mechain. One of his poems, 'Cywydd y gal' (Penis poem) was usually primly omitted from editions of his works – at least until recently.

The twelfth-century churchman Gerald of Wales was shocked by the shameless sexuality of his countrymen, 'Incest is very common among the Welsh,' he wrote. To be fair, his definition of incest was wider than it is now. 'They have no hesitation or shame in marrying women related to them in the fourth or fifth degree – and sometimes even third cousins.'

Such libertinage echoes down the centuries. In the First World War, women in Cardiff risked arrest if they were on the streets between 7 p.m. and 8 a.m. It was feared that their charms would detract from the war effort.

40

Because a Welshman was once described as 'the greatest living poet in the English language'

Dylan Thomas was born in Swansea in 1914. He showed early talent as a poet. His poem, 'Do Not Go Gentle Into that Good Night', published in 1933, has been voted the second most popular English poem. 'And Death Shall Have No Dominion', published the same year, repeats a theme of scorn for the Grim Reaper. There is magic in Thomas's choice of words and the way he chooses to weave them. This is well illustrated in his radio play *Under Milk Wood*, commissioned by the BBC and broadcast in 1954, ' ... Down to the sloeblack, slow, black, crowblack, fishingboatbobbing sea. The houses are blind as moles (though moles see fine to-night in the snouting velvet dingles') ... ' The play was later filmed, starring Richard Burton and Elizabeth Taylor. *Under Milk Wood* has been translated into more than thirty languages. Sadly, Dylan's early death in New York in 1953 – possibly from iatrogenic causes – deprived future generations of his enchanting verbal embroidery. The academic R.B. Kershner describes Thomas as, 'The Celtic bard with the magical rant, a folk figure with racial access to roots of experience which more civilized Londoners lacked.' The writer Philip Toynbee reviewed his *Collected Poems* and stated, 'Thomas is the greatest living poet in the English language.' For English-speakers, he is the mystic Welshman with the power to ensorcell with words. His prose work *A Child's Christmas in Wales*, is enchanting. His birthplace at 5 Cwmdonkin Drive in Swansea is visited by large numbers of his international admirers. You can even stay there overnight.

41

Because England's greatest writer may well have derived some inspiration from his close connections to Welsh people

William Shakespeare had Welsh ancestry through his grandmother, Alys Griffin. The Griffins themselves – as did the Tudors – traced their ancestry to Cadwaladr Fendigaid, Saint Cadwaladr the Blessed, the last British king, who died in AD 681. Some have posited that Shakespeare's plays show some infusion of Celtic oral poetic traditions. Shakespeare's teacher at King Edward VI Grammar School in Stratford-upon-Avon, Thomas Jenkins, was also Welsh. Stratford-upon-Avon had a significant Welsh population in Shakespeare's time.

Shakespeare had Welsh patrons, including the Earls of Pembroke and the Herberts, and was, of course, performing for and hoping to please Queen Elizabeth I, the last Tudor monarch, said by David Starkey, the historian, to be a Welsh speaker, and proud of her own Welsh roots (even A.N. Wilson admits she knew 'some Welsh' and pays tribute to her 'Welsh canniness'). Some of his actors were Welsh. Two of his plays, *King Lear* and *Cymbeline*, seem to derive their plots from old Welsh tales. Shakespeare exhibits a deep-seated and instinctive feel for the Welsh character, and all his Welsh characters are generously described: Henry V, born in Monmouth, is 'a mirror of all Christian kings'; Henry VII, the first Tudor king, is 'England's hope'; Glendower in *Henry IV*, is affable, brave and 'a worthy gentleman' and 'that great magician'; Fluellen in *Henry V* is loyal, chivalrous and trusty; and, Sir Hugh Evans in *The Merry Wives of Windsor* is peaceful and pious. In a wonderful juxtaposition of Welsh mysticism and northern English grounded bluntness, Shakespeare has these lines in *Henry IV*:

> Glendower: I can call spirits from the vasty deep.
> Hotspur: Why, so can I; or so can any man:
> But will they come, when you do call for them?

42

Because Welsh is the oldest living European language, pre-dating English by hundreds of years, bilingualism in English and Welsh is on the rise, and a Welsh substratum of history once extended well beyond the curtilage of Wales

Toby Young, writing in *The Spectator* on 13 September 2014, implied that there were insufficient vowels in the Welsh language: 'What have they got against vowels?' He should have checked his facts. Welsh has more vowels than English. Mr Young went on to mimic the translation into Welsh of the Hay Literary Festival as 'Gwg Ktghrsfg Brwyklnm' to give it its proper Welsh name'. This is proffered as a joke, we suppose, since the Welsh translation is 'Gŵyl Lenyddol y Gelli'. It is true that learning Welsh for English monoglot adults is difficult – the word orders in English and Welsh are different and the pronounciations of some letters are challenging. The other bugbear is that in English the wording does not flex very much – Welsh words can vary at the beginning and end and are subject to 'mutations' depending on what comes before. So, for instance, Cardiff is 'Caerdydd' in Welsh and in is 'yn' but 'in Cardiff' flexes to become 'yng Nghaerdydd'. Our suggestion to

English monoglots determined to master the challenge is to take an intensive wlpan course based on the methods the Israelis use to teach Jewish immigrants Hebrew and by which a dead language was fully revived. With a Welsh wlpan course, the committed learner will start dreaming in Welsh within weeks.

Even great Welsh patriots make mistakes. Saunders Lewis, poet, academic and playwright, delivered a withering speech, 'Tynged yr Iaith' (The Fate of the Language) on BBC radio in 1962. It was a speech pessimistic about the fate of the Welsh language, 'I shall also presuppose that Welsh will end as a living language, should the present trend continue, about the beginning of the twenty-first century.' His analysis was wrong but it did stimulate Welsh speakers to campaign for its revival. 'Cymdeithas yr Iaith Gymraeg', the Welsh Language Society, was formed later that year, and 'Mudiad Ysgolion Meithrin' (the Welsh Nursery School Movement) followed in 1971. The enthusiasm and commitment of Welsh-speaking teachers was key because when the aspirational monoglot English parents in Wales realised that high-quality public education in Wales was delivered in Welsh medium schools, the tide of battle was turned. From but one Welsh medium secondary school in Wales in 1956, there are now fifty catering for about 23 per cent of all secondary school pupils. When Saunders spoke, there were some 650,000 Welsh speakers in Wales. His pessimistic prediction proved to be way off the mark. In 2020, there were some 862,000 Welsh speakers in Wales. Bilingualism is on the rise, and the old chestnut that Welsh displaces other learning from the curriculum is rarely heard these days.

The Welsh National Anthem, *Hen Wlad fy Nhadau*, composed in 1856, took a boldly optimistic view of the future of the language in the third verse: 'Mae hen iaith y Cymry mor fyw ag erioed'. An English translation would be: 'The old language of the Welsh is as alive as ever'.

The Welsh language did not originate in Wales but in northern England and southern Scotland. Welsh – 'Yr hen iaith' – is the oldest living European language. Welsh bards were composing heroic and stirring epic verse, understandable to Welsh speakers today, some 800 years before anything recognisable as English was widely used by the English peasantry. For instance, there is a poem, 'Y Gododdin', written in the sixth century by Aneirin, which talks of Celtic Welsh warriors living along the banks of the Firth of Forth, and travelling 150 miles south to go into battle at Catterick in Yorkshire:

Gwyr a aeth Gatraeth oed fraeth eu llu
Glasved eu hancwyn a gwenwyn vu.
Trichant trwy beiryant eu cattau.
A gewedy elwch tawelch vu.

The men that went to Catterick were in fine fettle.
Their ration was rough mead – and was poison too.
300 went to battle, told what to do,
but after the shouting, silence did settle.

Sadly, they got badly drunk at a feast the night before the battle and, burdened with massive hangovers, they were duly slaughtered the next day. The Celtic habit of celebrating a victory prematurely persists to this day, as does the capacity to acquire a hangover. This battle was probably the defeat that cut off the southern Welsh speakers from those in the north ('Yr Hen Ogledd').

The historian, Norman Davies, in his book *Vanished Kingdoms*, discusses the persistence of Brythonic, P-Celtic, Cumbric, proto-Welsh in 'Alt Clud', the Kingdom of Strathclyde also known as the 'Kingdom of the Rock', which he believes was, 'The longest living fragment of the Ancient Britons' stronghold in northern Britain,'

44

Because the world's best ingredient comes from a zoo in north Wales

Alison and David, two graduates from Bangor University, set up the renowned Anglesey Sea Zoo in 1983. As well as being a tourist attraction with 100,000 visitors a year, the zoo is also now run as a research and conservation centre. Since business was seasonal, the entrepreneurs started trying to think up ways of boosting their income in the winter months. They knew the seawater locally was very clean because the notably finicky seahorses on display in the zoo were breeding merrily, so they hit upon reviving an older tradition that had died out by then in Anglesey – the making of sea salt. To further improve on purity the seawater is first filtered through charcoal beds. The product has proved a great success and under the brand name of Halen Môn (Salt of Anglesey) it appears on top tables around the world – at royal weddings, during the London Olympics in 2012, at political summits and on Barack Obama's table. It is exported to twenty-two countries and available in eleven flavours. Fifty-minute tours of the production site are run regularly. On 14 March 2018, Halen Môn won the accolade of being the World's Best Ingredient at the World Food Innovation Awards.

45

Because 'the greatest American architect of all time' was very proud of his Welsh roots

Frank Lloyd Wright was born in Wisconsin in 1867. His mother, Hannah, came from Llandyssul in Wales. Even when she was pregnant, she predicted that Frank would become a designer of beautiful buildings; she decorated his nursery with engravings of cathedrals to nurture him in the art of design. Her prediction came true.

Lloyd Wright began working as a draftsman in Chicago in 1887; after the Great Fire of Chicago in 1871 there was plenty of architectural work about. In 1893, he set up his own practice and his concept of 'organic architecture' flourished. Organic architecture envisages buildings blending in with their environment while at the same time being tailored to their intended function. In this he derived inspiration from his Welsh immigrant grandfather, Richard Lloyd Jones, who was described as follows: 'He was in league with the stones of the field ... the valley blossomed like a garden. His New Wales. He planted a small world within the world ... '

Lloyd Wright was very conscious of his Welsh roots. His adopted motto was 'Y gwir yn erbyn y Byd' – the truth against the world. He named the Wisconsin home he designed for himself 'Taliesin' after a legendary Welsh bard and set up the Taliesin Foundation to foster architectural talent. His most famous buildings are Fallingwater near Pittsburgh (known as 'the Building of the Twentieth Century') and the earthquake-proof Imperial Hotel in Tokyo. Some 532 of his buildings were constructed, the majority of which still stand. A third of his buildings are either situated in a National Historic District or are on the USA's National Register of Historic Places. Eight of them are on UNESCO's list of World Heritage Sites.

46

Because three geniuses of Welsh parentage changed the face of London forever

Inigo Jones was born in Smithfield to two Welsh-speaking teachers in 1573. He was sent to study drawing in Italy. From there he travelled to Denmark, where he worked for King Christian IV on the design of Frederiksborg Palace and Rosenborg Castle. Back home he made his name designing costumes and stage scenery, introducing movable scenery. He is credited with the introduction of the proscenium arch to English theatre. In 1615, his architectural skills were recognised in his appointment as Surveyor of the King's Works. He worked on Queen's House in Greenwich (between 1617 and its completion in 1635), Banqueting House, St Paul's Cathedral, the Covent Garden Piazza and Lincoln's Inn. More than 1,000 houses are attributed to him as architect. There is a bridge in Llanrwst, north Wales, that is called Pont Fawr, also known locally as Pont Inigo Jones (Inigo Jones's Bridge). In 1621, Jones was elected Member of Parliament for New Shoreham in West Sussex, and sat until the dissolution of Parliament in February 1622. Jones is regarded as the Founder of Classical English Architecture and the Greatest of English Renaissance artists. He is buried in the Welsh Church of the City of London.

John Nash was born in Lambeth in 1752, the son of a Welsh millwright. He left London for Carmarthen and it was in Wales that he developed his abilities as an architect. He designed three prisons: Carmarthen, Cardigan and Hereford. In 1797, he moved back to London. Under the patronage of the Prince Regent, he completed several major commissions: Regent Street, Carlton House Terrace, St James's Park, the Royal Pavilion in Brighton, the Regent's Canal, Buckingham Palace, the Royal Mews, Marble Arch and the Theatre Royal, Haymarket.

Hugh Myddelton was born in 1560 at Galch Hill in Denbighshire. He went to seek his fortune in London and, after being apprenticed in the trade, he became so successful that he was appointed Royal Jeweller by King James I. In addition, he himself became an MP, and he traded as a banker, miner (he ran lead and silver mines in Ceredigion), clothmaker, and engineer. London needed clean water to drink; the Thames was an open sewer. It was as an engineer that he became the driving force behind a major project to deliver a new source of clean water to the capital. This involved the construction of a new 38-mile channel from the River Lea near Ware to supply water to the new River Head in London. The project lasted from 1608 to 1613. He funded much of this himself. The king recognised his achievement in 1622 by making him a baronet. Amidst his portfolio of activities, he somehow found time to sire ten sons and six daughters.

47

Because a dexterous Welsh composer has broken all records in the classical charts

Karl Jenkins was born in Penclawdd on the Gower Coast in February 1944. He studied music in Cardiff University then at the Royal Academy of Music in London. In 1972, he joined the progressive rock band Soft Machine, which in 1974 was voted best small group in Melody Maker's jazz poll. His breakthrough as a composer came with his *Adiemus* project, a choral work, which he wrote in 1994. His album, *The Adiemus: Songs of Sanctuary*, released in 1995, topped the classical album charts. The life and teachings of St David inspired him to create his choral work *Dewi Sant* in 1999. In April 2000, his *The Armed Man*, based on the Catholic mass, premiered at the Royal Albert Hall. The work was commissioned by the Royal Armouries Museum for the Millennium celebrations. In the 1980s and '90s he was much involved with writing music for advertisements, for which he won two Design & Art Direction (D&AD) Awards. In 2008, *The Armed Man* was listed as No. 1 in Classic FM's Top 10 by living composers. In 2023, it broke all previous records by being in the classical music charts for more than 1,000 weeks. Jenkins is one of the most performed living composers today. His records have been certified either gold or platinum more than sixteen times. His output has been prolific and remarkably diverse, ranging from jazz, New Age and film music to classical. In 2015, Jenkins was knighted – he was the first Welsh composer to receive this honour. His work Tros y Garreg ('Over the Stone') was part of the musical programme performed before the Coronation of King Charles III.

Jenkins is very proud of being Welsh and thinks the Welsh are 'a cut above the rest of the UK when it comes to the ability to sing in four-part harmony'. He regrets he did not learn to speak Welsh when he was at school.

48

Because Wales boasts the largest prehistoric copper mines in the world

In 2004, *The Guinness Book of Records* recognised the Great Orme mines as the largest prehistoric copper mines in the world, and they were clearly the source of a thriving international export trade. The Great Orme is a headland to the north-west of Llandudno in north Wales. The mines were discovered as late as 1987 during a landscaping project on the headland. About 5 miles of mining tunnels have been found so far — it is thought that half of the total mine has been excavated to date. This represents quite a technological achievement for miners equipped with only stone or bone tools. Some 3,000 tools have been found. The miners used fat candles for light during their mining. The copper ore malachite began to be worked here about 4,000 years ago in the Bronze Age. The heyday of the mines was between 1600 and 1400 BC. The copper produced must have been traded widely because the fingerprint of its isotopes has been found in objects in France, Germany and Sweden. One conservative estimate puts the amount of copper mined as 1,760 tonnes — enough to fashion at least 200 million artefacts. Mining was resumed on the Great Orme in the late seventeenth century and indeed it was referred to as the Welsh California in the 1840s. The mines were abandoned — for the second time in history — in 1881. The site is open to the tourist public from March to October.

49

Because Welsh gold, used for the wedding rings of royalty, can be worth up to 30 times the world value of gold

Mining for Welsh gold has a long history. The Romans mined it at Dolaucothi in Carmarthenshire between AD 75 and 300. Modern mining ceased there in 1938, but it can be visited as a tourist attraction.

Gwynfynydd gold mine near Ganllwyd, Dolgellau, in Gwynedd, was discovered in 1860 and remained active until 1998, when it was closed owing to health and safety concerns regarding the discharge from the mine into the River Mawddach. It is estimated that in 2017 terms the mine produced £44 million worth of gold. Gold from the Gwynfynydd mine was used in the Glyndŵr Award, which is presented annually for excellence in the arts in Wales. Previous medal winners include the painter Sir Kyffin Williams; the author Jan Morris; the composer Alun Hoddinott; and the poet Gillian Clarke. A kilogram of Gwynfynydd gold was also used for a present to the late Queen Elizabeth II on her sixtieth birthday.

The tradition of using Welsh gold in the wedding rings of the British Royal family began when Lady Elizabeth Bowes-Lyon married the Duke of York (later King George VI) on 26 April 1923. Princess Elizabeth and Philip Mountbatten married on 20 November

1947 at Westminster Abbey. Her wedding ring was crafted from a nugget of pure Welsh gold from the Clogau mine. The tradition continues – both Catherine, Princess of Wales, and Meghan, Duchess of Sussex, wear wedding rings of Welsh gold.

No gold is currently being mined in Wales. Nevertheless, at present, Welsh gold can be valued up to thirty times more than standard world gold because of its scarcity value.

50

Because legend has it that Joseph of Arimathea brought the Holy Grail to Britain and is buried in the Riverside area of Cardiff

In AD 33, Jesus and his disciples had a last Passover supper together. Each man present took four cups of wine, but they all shared Jesus's wine from Jesus's cup, and this forms the basis of the service of Holy Communion worldwide. This cup, later rechristened the Holy Grail, has acquired many a layer of legend. There are at least 200 objects in Europe purporting to be the Holy Grail – and Wales has its own, the Nant Eos cup. What's more, this cup is reputed to have powers to heal the person drinking from it. This venerated object found its way for safekeeping to the Cistercian abbey of Strata Florida in Cardiganshire. In his desire to exercise his loins, Henry VIII fell out with the Pope and decided to dissolve the monasteries as outposts of Papal authority. In 1539, the last few monks of Strata Florida escaped with the Grail before their abbey was destroyed and their treasure impounded. They managed to secrete it in a mansion nearby, Nant Eos. It survived fire, theft and occasional attempts by users to nibble the wood for curative purposes. It is now on display in the National Library of Wales in Aberystwyth.

St Joseph of Arimathea was a wealthy man who paid for the burial shroud and tomb for Jesus. He became connected with the legend of

King Arthur, and some say he was the first keeper of the Holy Grail. The Rev. Sabine Baring-Gould retold a Cornish tale that had Joseph visiting Cornwall accompanied by his nephew, the boy Jesus. Joseph is also depicted as a tin merchant prospecting in Cornwall. Others say he brought the Holy Grail to Britain and this is connected with the Nant Eos cup.

The ruler Maelgwn of Llandaff, a church benefactor, related that Joseph was buried in the curtilage of an old church alongside the River Taff. The author Michael A. Clark places the grave, intact and in the open within the remains of the Chapel of St Mary, in Bute Park, Cardiff. One wonders whether the saint acquired a Cardiff accent before he passed.

51

Because two international icons of fashion in the twentieth century had Welsh roots

Mary Quant was born in London in 1930, the daughter of two Welsh teachers. She was raised in Pembrokeshire. Her talent was designing and fashion. She once stated, 'Fashion is a tool to compete in life outside the home.' In 1955, she opened the trendy boutique Bazaar in Chelsea, west London. She rode the crest of the fashion wave in the 1960s, offering youthful, edgy fashion concentrating on young women. She was one of the leaders in popularising, if not inventing, miniskirts and hotpants. Many of her clothes were manufactured in Pontypridd in south Wales. On 15 October 1963, she won the Sunday Times Fashion Award. In 1965, it was estimated that she was producing 528 designs a year. In the 1970s and '80s she branched out into household items and make-up. In 1990, she won the Hall of Fame Award of the British Fashion Council. In 2000, she sold her make-up business to a Japanese concern, and there are some 200 Mary Quant colour shops in Japan. She was made a Dame Commander of the Order of the British Empire in 2015. In 2020, the V&A ran a special exhibition of the work of this Swinging Sixties icon.

Laura Mountney was born in Merthyr Tydfil in 1925 and married Bernard Ashley in 1949. She began designing Victorian-style headscarves in 1953. Laura Ashley opened her first shop in Machynlleth in 1963, where they sold their clothing products together with local honey and walking sticks. The company moved into an old railway station in Carno in 1963 with a 3,600ft extension. Her business grew exponentially; the family could afford a private plane, a yacht, the French Château de Remaisnil in Picardy, a townhouse in Brussels, and the Villa Contenta in New Providence, Bahamas. The business had global reach by the mid-80s and employed 4,000 people in 220 stores worldwide. It grossed about $130 million a year in revenue. Sadly, Laura died in 1985. A few months after her death, Laura Ashley went public with the shares thirty-four times oversubscribed. In 2018, the company won the Best Licensed Lifestyle Brand Award. Although the business went into administration in 2020, it relaunched in partnership with Next in 2021. *The New York Times* said of her, 'With her floral-print dresses and housewares, the British designer created a romantic and instantly recognisable aesthetic that, decades later, is inspiring a wide range of dressers and brands.'

52

Because south Wales backed the most inspirational expedition in polar history that laid the foundations of modern science on Antarctica[2]

For his attempt to reach the South Pole, Robert Falcon Scott managed to get the backing of a number of Cardiff businessmen, and that was the reason his expedition set off from Cardiff. Scott was given a fine send-off at a dinner with them and the Lord Mayor in the Alexandra Room of the Royal Hotel on 13 June 1910. Scott gave a thank you speech saying that the expedition, 'could not have faced the strain of preparation except for the support they had received from south Wales'. Indeed, Cardiff was the leading provider of funds within the UK. Lieutenant Edward Evans, who played a key role in drumming up Cardiff's enthusiasm, recorded his pleasure: 'Free docking, free coal, defects (of the vessel) made good for nothing, an office and staff placed at our disposal, in fact everything was done with an open-handed generosity.' The free docking and fuel were estimated at a 1915 value of £5,000 (equivalent to £738,000 in 2024).

Scott stayed as a guest of honour in the Mansion House in The Walk before he left: this was the building that later became an ortho-

---

2   According to the Antarctic Heritage Trust.

The whaling ship *Terra Nova*, converted for polar exploration.

paedic hospital inspired by John Lynn-Thomas (see Reasons 61 & 83). The crew were given dinner on the same night by the Chamber of Commerce at Barry's Hotel, also located in St Mary Street. They joined the officers and Scott in the rather posher Royal Hotel for entertainment after the dinner.

Before leaving, Scott's ship, the *Terra Nova*, took on coal and 'patent fuel' in the docks in Cardiff. Some 200 tonnes of coal were donated, half by the Ynyshir Colliery Company and half by Messrs Insole and Sons. Patent fuel was coal combined with bitumen moulded into briquette shapes for use in ships' boilers. It had several advantages over coal – it took up 30 per cent less space, and it was more resistant than ordinary coal to the depredations of extreme cold. The Crown Patent Fuel Company made a gift of 300 tonnes of patent fuel to the *Terra Nova*. South Wales was famous for its rectangular blocks of patent fuel, varying between 9 and 26lb each in weight. Scott was later to use his ingenuity and stack these rectangular blocks to build stable shelters in the frozen wastes. They may well still be there, a touching testimony to south Wales's proud industrial past.

Scott left Cardiff with leeks tied to the mast of his ship on 15 June 1910, and with the Red Dragon Flag, a gift from the Cardiff draper James Howell, streaming proudly from the mizzen. The Cardiff Flag presented to Scott by the Lord Mayor flew at the fore. Tryggve Gran, the Norwegian skiing expert, who sailed with Scott, described the day:

> Neither before or since in time of peace have I heard such an uproar as that which made the air tremble as Terra Nova glided out of the docks. People in their thousands yelled as if they had taken leave of their senses. Railway waggons were rolled over a line covered with dynamite detonators, and vessels in their hundreds completed the noise with whistles and sirens. At the last lock gates we were met by a little squadron of beflagged boats and with this as escort we steamed out into the open sea.

Scott, who prophesied, 'I will reach the South Pole or I will never come back again,' returned ashore on the tug *Falcon*. Scott carried on with some extra fundraising in the UK before taking a mail steamer to meet up with and join the *Terra Nova* in Simonstown, South Africa.

After much difficulty, Scott reached the South Pole on 18 January 1912. 'Great God, this is an awful place,' he wrote simply yet tellingly, 'and terrible enough for us to have laboured without the reward of priority.' Scott was surely depressed because the Norwegians under Amundsen had got there first a month before on 15 December 1911. Scott had no choice but to try to return to base. The weather conditions were awful. The Welsh Petty Officer Edgar Evans was the first to die, badly affected by frostbite. His body has never been found. Captain Lawrence Oates, himself badly frostbitten in his hands and feet, had been slowing the party and on 16 March he nobly left the group, remarking as he left the tent, 'I am just going outside and may be some time.' He never returned. His brave self-sacrifice was in vain. Scott very nearly made it back to base, but some time in late March 1912 his party ran out of provisions and ran into a severe nine-day snowstorm only 11 miles from safety. His last diary entry was dated 29 March, presumably his day of death.

On 12 November 1912, Scott was found dead with two of his remaining companions. They left their diaries behind them. Scott wrote, 'Had we lived, I should have a tale to tell of the hardihood, endurance, and courage of my companions which would have stirred the heart of every Englishman. These rough notes and our dead bodies must tell the tale.'

The *Terra Nova*'s figurehead with flowing blonde hair and white summery dress fringed in blue.

The lighthouse in Roath Park contains a scale model of the *Terra Nova*.

The industrialist F.C. Bowring agreed to donate the figurehead of the ship as a memorial to Scott and to reside in Roath Park (she now blushes unseen in store in the National Museum of Wales).

This formal presentation took place on 8 December 1913. During the ceremony Mr Bowring promised that he would provide funds to construct a memorial clock tower in addition to the figurehead. The clocktower, in the form of a lighthouse at the south end of Roath Park Lake, was finished in January 1915. The lighthouse, commonly pictured on postcards of the city, has now become almost more of a symbol of Cardiff than of Scott.

The Alexandra Room in the Royal Hotel was later renamed The Captain Scott Room. The Captain Scott Society was founded in this room in 1982. It makes two annual awards to encourage the spirit of adventure. The Society donated the *Terra Nova*'s binnacle for public display in Cardiff.

53

Because there is an argument that without the achievements of Welsh men there would be no USA

In 1497, John Cabot set sail from Bristol on his ship *The Matthew*. The owner of the ship, and funder of the expedition, was the Welsh trader Richard ap Meurig, who hailed from Chepstow. His name was anglicised to Richard Amerike (*c*.1440–1503). There are claims that he funded the expedition on the basis of a promise that any newly found land would be named after him. This was Cabot's second voyage and although he thought he had reached Asia, he actually landed on Newfoundland. The ap Meurig coat of arms features stars and stripes – as indeed does the US national flag. Most experts seem to hold the questionable theory that America is named after the Italian explorer Amerigo Vespucci, though he certainly never named any land 'America'; what is more, the evidence that he made westward voyages of exploration depends nearly entirely on a handful of letters he is said to have written. Diffie and Winius, in their book *Foundations of the Portuguese Empire 1415–1580*, state, 'Historians have differed sharply on the authorship, accuracy and veracity of these documents.' There is no good evidence that he ever made landfall in north America. Ralph Waldo Emerson wrote Vespucci off as a 'pickle dealer at Seville ... whose highest naval rank was boatswain's mate in an expedition that never sailed'. It is far more romantic – at least if you are Welsh – to credit a Welsh man with the origin of the word 'America'.

Welsh financing skill made America independent. Robert Morris was born in Liverpool in January 1734. The Pennsylvania House of Representatives recognises him as of Welsh descent. He emigrated to the USA, where he made his fortune in shipping. By 1775, he was the richest man in America. He served as a member of the Pennsylvania legislature, the Second Continental Congress, and the United States Senate. His was the second signature on the Declaration of Independence, and he signed the Articles of Confederation and the United States Constitution (he was one of only two men to sign all three documents). From 1781 to 1784, he served as the Superintendent of Finance of the United States, and is recognised as the 'Financier of the Revolution' – in 1775 he was financing and facilitating the smuggling of gunpowder to Washington's forces. As Superintendent of Finance, he used his own funds to sustain the Continental Army and to reassure foreign allies about lines of credit. Congress had no power at that time to levy taxes. US Founding Father Alexander Hamilton said of Morris, 'I believe no man in this country but himself could have kept the money machine a-going.' He is widely acknowledged as one of the founders of the financial system of the United States.

54

Because the daughters of the American Revolution believe that a Welsh prince discovered America

Ieuan Ddu was born in 1527. He is better known by his anglicised name of John Dee. His family had its roots in Powys and, indeed, he claimed descent from the great Welsh king Rhodri Mawr. He was a clever polymath, an early young meteor. He graduated from St John's College, Cambridge, as early as 1544. Aged 23, he found himself lecturing in mathematics in Paris 'to enormous acclaim'. His all-round abilities propelled him towards royal recognition by the Tudor queen Elizabeth I. He became a royal adviser at court, court astronomer and court astrologer. He was a strong advocate for a national library and for colonisation of north America, and he established a claim for the British throne on the basis that Prince Madoc from Wales had discovered America about AD 1170.

Madoc left north Wales with 300 men and thirteen ships from Llandrillo-yn-Rhos (where there is a plaque that marks his departure) and according to some, discovered America. The Daughters of the American Revolution have set up a plaque in Mobile, Alabama, that reads, 'In Memory of Prince Madoc who landed on the shores of Mobile Bay in 1170 and left behind, with the Indians, the Welsh language'. Dee is even credited with minting the term 'British Empire'. His knowledge of navigation was such that he had a hand in guiding explorers on England's voyages of discovery. He foresaw great potential in the future for Elizabeth's empire based on the protection of a strong navy. His advocacy of such projection of power left indelible marks on British and American history. He was imbued with elements of Welsh mysticism that led some to think he summoned up spirits and his library, once the finest in England, was sadly vandalised by his detractors.

Persistent tales of Indians who spoke or understood Welsh provoked the third President of the United States and author of the American Declaration of Independence, Thomas Jefferson, of Welsh descent and who believed the Madoc story to be correct, to ask the Lewis and Clark expedition to find the descendants of the Welsh Madoc Indians. Accordingly, in 1803, Lewis (of Welsh extraction himself) and Clark set off on their expedition. Lewis and Clark effectively opened up the American West, and members of the expedition reported meeting light-skinned Indians who were from this lost Welsh tribe mouthing a 'gurgling kind of language spoken much through the throat'.

It is commonly held that the Mandan Indians were Madoc's descendants. They were amiable and chopsy. Besides, they had coracles. Some were blond and had blue eyes. There are indeed some linguistic convergences – head in Mandan is 'pan' (Welsh = pen) and house is 'teew' (Welsh = tŷ).

55

Because the USA owes its independent existence to the agitation of a maltster of Welsh descent

In 1773, the Boston Tea Party took place in protest against the British government conceding a monopoly of importation of tea into America, undercutting local tea merchants and tea smugglers. The rebels' target was the Tea Act of 1773. The reverberations of this event led to the American Revolution and ultimately to the foundation of the United States of America. One instigator of the Boston Tea Party and organiser of the 'Sons of Liberty' was Samuel Adams, who had previously campaigned vociferously against British taxation without the colonialists being represented in the British Parliament. He was a maltster of Welsh descent. He was a failure in business, but a successful revolutionary in politics. He – together with as many as seventeen other men of Welsh descent – was a signatory of the Declaration of Independence for the thirteen American colonies. He remained a member of the Continental Congress until 1781, where he helped draft the Articles of Confederation. After the Revolution, Sam became Governor of Massachusetts between 1794 and 1797, but it was as 'the Greatest Incendiary in the Empire' that he is better remembered. His health is toasted in modern Samuel Adams beer brewed by the Boston Brewing Company. Thomas Jefferson recognised his central role as 'truly the Man of the Revolution'. He died in 1803.

56

Because at least twelve American presidents had Welsh ancestry

Five of the six first presidents of the USA had Welsh pedigrees. In total, at least twelve presidents – so far – had Welsh antecedents: Adams, father and son; Thomas Jefferson; James Madison; James Monroe; William Henry Harrison; Abraham Lincoln; James Garfield; Benjamin Harrison; Calvin Coolidge; Richard Nixon; and Barack Obama.

In hindsight, some of the earlier presidents on this list are tainted by association with slavery. Abraham Lincoln, president between 1861 and 1865, dilutes this criticism in that he was to promote the 13th Amendment to the US Constitution, which was to abolish slavery shortly after his assassination in 1865. As Commander in Chief during the Civil War, he proved a highly competent strategist. His great grandmother, Ellen James, had emigrated to America from Wales (she was from Ysbyty Ifan in north Wales). In the US she married Cadwalader Evans from Ucheldre near Bala. Lincoln was sufficiently aware of the importance of the Welsh vote that in 1860 he had 100,000 election pamphlets printed in Welsh.

In 1797, John Adams, of Welsh descent, became the second US president and served till 1801. He was the first US president to enter the White House. He is also the only one of the first twelve presidents not to have owned slaves. The Adams family's ancestral home was Penybanc Farm, near Llanboidy in west Carmarthenshire.

Adams proposed Washington as Commander in Chief for the War of Independence and in 1779 he negotiated the peace settlement with England to end the war under the Treaty of Paris. He was one of the drafters and signatories of the Declaration of Independence and argued fiercely in its favour before Congress finally accepted it on 2 July 1776. He had been twice vice president under George Washington. Some regard him as 'the Father of the American Navy' because he built up America's naval power in anticipation of potential conflict with Revolutionary France.

Thomas Jefferson became the third president in 1801 and served until 1809. He, too, was one of the drafters and signatories of the Declaration of Independence. His father came from the Snowdon area. A US State Department official unveiled a plaque in 1933 at Llanfair Careinion inscribed with, 'To the Memory of a Great Welshman, Thomas Jefferson'. As president in 1803, he negotiated and signed the Louisiana Purchase of 600 million acres of land from France at the bargain price of 3 cents an acre, $15 million in total – not a bad price for doubling the size of the United States. He also initiated and won the First Barbary War against Barbary Corsairs, leading to the release of 115 Americans from slavery – hence the reference to the 'shores of Tripoli' in the first verse of the Marines' Hymn. Thomas Jefferson also read, spoke, and wrote Welsh – this is proven by his correspondence in Welsh with Meriwether Lewis, his aide. On retiring from office, Jefferson founded the University of Virginia.

On his maternal side, James Madison had Welsh roots through the Gaines family. He was a Founding Father of the USA and became the first Secretary of State between 1801 and 1809, and fourth President of the USA between 1809 and 1817. He is known as 'the Father of the Constitution' for his key role in drafting and promoting the Constitution of the United States and the Bill of Rights.

James Monroe was another 'Founding Father' who became president. As the fifth President of the USA, he served between 1817 and 1825. His grandfather on his maternal side, James Jones, an architect, had emigrated from Wales. He is best known for the 'Monroe Doctrine' that sought to limit European colonialism in the New World. He also came to terms with and settled various border disputes with the British.

John Adams' son, John Quincy Adams, became sixth President of the USA between 1825 and 1829. As Secretary of State in 1817 he had negotiated the Adams-Onis Treaty that acquired Florida from Spain. His ambitious plans for the presidency were largely blocked by Congress, though he did manage to secure support for various infrastructure improvements.

57

Because Wales has produced a cracking crop of comedians

Nancy Reagan called Bob Hope, 'America's most honored citizen and our favorite clown'. Bob Hope's 'Mam', Iris Towns, was Welsh and she married William Hope in Cardiff in April 1891. They lived in Barry and Newport, and later moved to England, where Bob was born in May 1903. He made a name for himself in the USA as a comedian and film star. In all, he was awarded more than 2,000 awards and fifty-four honorary university doctorates. In October 1984, he returned to the old family home at 12 Greenwood Street in Barry to unveil a blue plaque on the house in his family's honour.

Thomas Cooper, the son of a miner, was born in Caerphilly in 1922. When he was 8 years old, an aunt bought him a magic set and he spent hours playing with the tricks. He became a skilled magician and eventually became a member of the Magic Circle's Inner Six. However, he discovered that he could entertain people more with his humour based on his magic tricks going wrong. He made his TV debut in 1947 in Leslie Henson's *Christmas Party*. Tommy Cooper, with his trademark fez, was named ITV Personality of the Year in 1969. He had various runs of TV shows and appeared several times on the *Ed Sullivan Show* in the USA. He collapsed on stage during a live performance of *Live From Her Majesty's* in April 1984 but the audience laughed, thinking it was part of the act. It wasn't – he had a heart attack and died 'just like that'. A statue of Cooper was unveiled in his birthplace, Caerphilly, in 2008 by fellow Welshman Sir Anthony Hopkins, who is patron of the Tommy Cooper Society. In a 2005 poll, 'The Comedians' Comedian', comedians and comedy insiders voted Cooper the sixth greatest comedy act ever.

Rob Brydon was born in 1965 in Baglan, Glamorganshire. He showed an early talent for acting at school in Porthcawl and afterwards spent a year at the Royal Welsh College of Music and Drama in Cardiff. He began work at Radio Wales aged 20 and his career sprang from there. He is multi-talented – a disc jockey, impressionist (notably of Tom Jones, Mick Jagger and Richard Burton), West End stage actor, comedian, presenter, voice-over artist, author, scriptwriter and singer. He is best known as a comedian and the role that catapulted him to fame was as Uncle Bryn in *Gavin and Stacey*. Uncle Bryn epitomises the essence of Welsh humour and portrays an amiable stock Welsh character. Brydon's comic relief single, '(Barry) Islands in the Stream', which he performed with Tom Jones, reached No. 1 in the UK charts on 15 March 2009. He has appeared in more than thirty films. He was awarded an MBE in 2013 for his services to comedy and broadcasting and for charitable services.

58

Because 'the pioneer of cinema' proudly claimed to be of Welsh royal descent

David Llewelyn Wark Griffith was born in Oldham County, Kentucky, in 1875. 'DW' proudly claimed his descendancy from Gruffudd ap Llewelyn, the only Welsh king to rule over the whole of Wales. Some have christened Griffith 'the Pioneer of Cinema' and others 'the Father of Film'. He made some 500 films in all, and he pioneered a variety of innovative techniques including masterful use of lighting, fade in/fade out, close up and cross-cutting. His famous films include *The Birth of a Nation*, *Intolerance*, *Hearts of the World*, *The Cricket on the Hearth*, *The Fall of Babylon* and *Broken Blossoms*. Together with Mary Pickford, Douglas Fairbanks and Charlie Chaplin, he founded United Artists in order to reduce the stranglehold of commercial studios over screen artists. He was hugely talented but had the unfortunate habit of overspending on productions, and after his production of *The Struggle* in 1931 he could not find finance to produce any more movies. He was commemorated on a US postal stamp in 1975; he has a star on the Hollywood Walk of Fame; and the Directors Guild of America used to bestow the D.W. Griffith Award as its highest honour.

59

Because the revival of commercial viticulture in Britain after the Middle Ages was a Welsh achievement

It is always enlightening when science and history prove themselves to be resilient enough to be rewritten in the light of facts discovered that challenge an accepted narrative.

The assertion that world climate change is primarily driven by fossil fuel emissions looks simplistic when we acknowledge the existence of cycles of Ice Ages and warmer periods (which cannot have had anything to do with industrialisation) or the fact that the Romans produced wine in Britain in large quantities. They had at least seven active vineyards in Britannia, one of them as far north as North Thoresby in Lincolnshire – 53° north. Viticulture here was proven by excavation and palynology, and it is thought the area would have produced 30,000 litres of white wine a year.

The climate appears to have been warmer than it subsequently became. In June 2020, after analysing marine contents, Spanish and Italian scientists published research in scientific journals indicating that the climate was 2°C warmer in the Roman period than it is now. 'For the first time, we can state the Roman period [AD 1 to AD 500] was the warmest period of time of the last 2,000 years, and these conditions lasted for 500 years,' according to Professor Isabel Cacho at the Department of Earth and Ocean Dynamics, University of Barcelona.

Wine making may have lingered on after the Romans left, but the fall in average temperatures and the Dissolution of the Monasteries under Henry VIII seems to have destroyed the industry for centuries.

It used to be thought by 'experts' that grapes for wine could not be grown commercially outside of the latitudes 30–50° north of the Equator. It is commonly asserted that Major General Sir Guy Salisbury-Jones was the first British person to challenge this orthodoxy. He planted vines in 1952 and in 1961 at Hambledon (51°N) 'which became the first winery in England to release a commercial vintage' (Criterion Wine Tours website).

The point is that the assertion is untrue because good wine was being produced in commercial quantities in Cardiff (51°N) from about 1885, and the true pioneer of viticulture in the UK was the 3rd Marquess of Bute more than six decades before Salisbury-Jones.

Bute grew grapes on the south-facing walls of Cardiff Castle and at three vineyards – Castell Coch/Tongwynlais; Swanbridge near Sully; and St Quentin near Cowbridge. For a number of years, his harvests were disappointing and the news that Europe's wealthiest young nobleman was setting out on such outlandish experiments provoked satire. *Punch* predicted that if ever wine was actually produced in south Wales, 'It would take four men to drink it – two to hold the victim down, and one to pour it down his throat!'

The vineyards eventually produced far more wine than the family required, and it was decided to market it commercially. The 1881 vintage was sold at 60*s* per dozen bottles, a large proportion of it being subsequently resold by public auction at 115*s* per dozen (a premium price – a full-bodied burgundy would cost about 24*s* per dozen at that time). The wine is described by connoisseurs as resembling a first-class still champagne. In 1897 Hatch, Mansfield and Co., a London firm of wine merchants, were given the agency for wine sales. 'A novelty, Welsh wines' announced their catalogue, which offered eight varieties, with prices ranging from 36*s* a dozen for the 1892 vintage, to 48*s* for the 1885 wines. They advertised four different types of Bute wine – 'Full Golden Rather Sweet, Dark Golden Medium Sweet, A Luscious Golden Wine and Light Golden 126 Mellow'. In 1893, Bute's vineyards yielded an enormous quantity of grapes, from which were pressed 40 hogsheads (2,640 gallons). The whole of it was sold by the Marquess under a licence held in his own name for a 'sum of £3,000, that one season's results recouping all the expenditure incurred upon the experiments up to that date' (*Weekly Mail*, 9 October 1897). After the 3rd Marquess died in 1900, his young son was equally enthusiastic about the vines, although he encountered a number of bad years. In 1905, a visitor noted 63,000 vines in cultivation but what killed off this nascent industry was the First World War and the shortage of sugar.

Decent red wine is harder to produce in more northern climes: there is some production of German red wine, but it is neither very memorable nor very substantial. Adam Lechmere, a wine expert, was reported in *The Guardian* in 2017 as saying, 'As for the UK, we just do not have the climate to ripen red grapes.' Well, Lord Bute did ripen red grapes, made a good red wine (in 1893) and sold it in quantity – but most of his production was, of course, white.

Nowadays, Vineyards of Wales lists thirty-three Welsh vineyards, one of them as far north as 53°N. Recently, Welsh vineyards have won more than twenty major awards including the Best Sparkling Wine in the World in 2012. Most of these vineyards produce red wine as part of their offering. A pinot noir red wine from Monmouthshire's White Castle became the first Welsh vintage to win a Gold Medal at the Decanter World Wine Awards in 2018. Bute's pioneering spirit lives on in defiance of received opinion.

60

Because modern-day banking has many roots in Wales

Should the Lloyd's Bank horse be black or grey? Much of modern banking has Welsh roots. The Welsh are careful with their money. On 30 October 1799, the Black Ox Bank was established successfully at Llandovery by David Jones, the son of a Welsh farmer. He died rich, and eventually the goodwill of the bank devolved on Lloyd's Bank in 1903. Lloyd's itself was partly founded by Sampson Lloyd, of Welsh Quaker stock in 1765. Lloyd derives from 'llwyd' (grey in Welsh) so maybe its horse ought to be grey.

In 1986, the Midland Bank celebrated the 150th anniversary of the North & South Wales Bank, once an extensive business. When the Wales Bank amalgamated with Midland in 1908, it was one of the largest provincial banks with more than 100 branches. The manager of the Cardigan branch in 1840–47 was a 'respectable' maltster (Cardigan had a reputation for smuggling), William Phillips, who married an ancestor of the authors. He is illustrated in the 1850s ambrotype. The Midland Bank was taken over by HSBC in 1999.

In 1827, the Pembrokeshire Bank was established in Haverfordwest by John and William Walters. Eventually, it was taken over by the London Provincial Bank in 1872. The Bank of Wales was set up in Swansea in 1863 and began opening branches across south Wales. The bank Lock, Hulm & Co. opened for business in Pembroke in 1834 before it was taken over by the Bank of Wales in 1864. All of these were eventually merged with Barclays Bank in 1918.

Sir Julian Hodge, a Cardiff financier, founded the Bank of Wales in 1971. It was taken over by the Bank of Scotland in 1986 and ceased trading under the Welsh brand in 2002.

The 'neobank' Starling, the first digital bank, was founded by Anne Boden, born in Swansea in 1960. It received its UK banking licence in 2016. The bank is paperless and branchless, and its current accounts have been voted Britain's best for five years. Its largest office in the UK is in Cardiff. Wales continues its tradition of banking innovation.

William Phillips, maltster and banker and his wife, Hannah.

61

Because a pragmatic Welsh tradition of bone-setting revolutionised orthopaedic surgery in the First World War

In 1743, in mysterious circumstances, a stormy sea threw up a 7-year-old boy speaking no English or Welsh by shipwreck on the shore of Anglesey. The castaway was adopted by a local doctor, who named him Evan Thomas. The boy was to demonstrate that he possessed remarkable – charmed almost – bone-setting abilities. He began a family line of Welsh bone-setters, enigmatic in origin, but pragmatically successful. His great grandson, Hugh Owen Thomas, born in 1834, broke from the family tradition somewhat by becoming properly medically qualified. He was to become known as 'the Father of Modern Orthopaedics' and invented a splint that was to reduce deaths dramatically after fracture among Liverpool dockers in the nineteenth century. His nephew, Sir Robert Jones, who had trained at Thomas's side, became Director of Military Orthopaedics in the First World War. In April 1916, Sir John Lynn-Thomas, born in Cwmgefeile near Llandysul in Cardiganshire, became Deputy Inspector of Military Orthopaedics, Western Command, on the recommendation of Sir Robert Jones. In this position, Lynn-Thomas was to revolutionise the treatment of femoral fractures in the First World War through his advocacy of the Thomas Splint.

Before 1917, treatment of femoral fractures was little short of barbaric with unacceptably high death rates (*c*.80 per cent) and it carried the risk all too often of lifelong disability even if the patient survived. The Thomas Splint reduced the death rate dramatically to 8 per cent. He also helped establish orthopaedics as a speciality of itself – overcoming professional conservatism that resisted any compartmentalisation of general surgery. Lynn-Thomas's pioneering massively advanced the treatment of orthopaedics worldwide and saved thousands of soldiers' lives.

Lynn-Thomas, orthopaedic pioneer.

62

Because a brave and pioneering Welsh doctor continues to advance the boundaries of war surgery in the twenty-first century

In 2020, David Nott received the Christopher Bland Award. This award is given by the Royal Society of Literature to encourage the work of older writers. Nott's award was as a result of his work, *War Doctor: Surgery on the Front Line*. Nott was born in Carmarthen in 1956. He was destined to become a consultant surgeon specialising in vascular and general surgery. In 1993, he began volunteering some weeks of his time in disaster areas and war zones. He has served in Afghanistan, Bosnia, Haiti, Chad, Gaza, Darfur, Sierra Leone, Iraq, Libya, Syria and even Ukraine. Between 2013 and 2014, in war-torn East Aleppo he began training other doctors and medical students to carry out trauma surgery. While in Libya he set up a 'Definitive Surgical Trauma Skills Initiative' workshop. He was to expand this concept into the David Nott Foundation in 2015 as a charitable foundation that promotes life-saving surgical techniques designed for use in emergencies and difficult and dangerous environments. In 2016, he won the Robert Burns Humanitarian Award and the Pride of Britain Award. He has been dubbed, 'the Indiana Jones of Surgery'. This brave Welshman has saved lives and relieved much suffering in dangerous and difficult circumstances and propagates his knowledge to others.

63

Because a pioneering Welsh surgeon lost the use of his right arm, learned how to operate with his left hand and significantly advanced war surgery in the Second World War

Hugh Morriston Davies was born in Swansea in 1879. Morriston is a suburb of Swansea. He went into medicine, and at the remarkably young age of 29 became head of surgical staff at University College Hospital. There he pioneered treatment for trigeminal neuralgia, but then specialised in diseases of the chest, notably tuberculosis. Tragically, especially for a surgeon, his right hand became infected following an operation. Amputation was recommended but the arm and hand were saved. However, the limb was left in a condition that was useless for surgery. Davies left surgery to run a sanatorium but, with remarkable resolution and application, he learned how to undertake surgery with his left hand and returned to the profession in 1921. He was acknowledged as an inspiring innovator in thoracic surgery and he was to become thoracic consultant to all Welsh hospitals. During the Second World War he published his seminal work, *War Injuries of the Chest*. Davies was the first person to diagnose a lung tumour by X-ray. Nowadays, there is a Scadding-Morriston Davies Joint Fellowship in Respiratory Medicine for British medical students interested in the speciality, named partly in his memory.

64

Because an eccentric Welsh doctor effectively legalised and set a fashion for cremation

Eccentric Welsh doctors truly deserve a place in history. Born in Rudry, William Price studied under Dr Evan Edwards in Caerphilly for six years and then surprised everyone by enrolling at the Royal College of Surgeons and passing the necessary medical examinations in a record twelve months. He returned to Wales to practise. He could speak Hindi fluently, proclaimed himself as an Archdruid and started building a druidic temple. His medical practice emphasised preventative medicine; he was firmly against purging and bleeding and the smoking of tobacco. He was, however, an anti-vaxxer. He was a supporter of increased democracy through the Chartist movement and attended their rallies in a cart drawn by goats. He believed in free love and in his sixty-sixth year began a relationship with a 21-year-old, Gwenllian. She gave him a son in his eighty-third year and they named him Iesu Grist (Jesus Christ). The poor baby died at only five months old. In 1884, Price shocked the locals when he tried to cremate his son on a mountain top in Llantrisant. He was arrested and his court case began in February 1884 in Cardiff. Price argued that, although the law did not say cremations were legal, it did not say they were illegal either. The judge agreed with him. Price himself was cremated and his funeral ceremony was the first legal cremation in Britain on 31 January 1893. He started a fashion: cremation is by far the most popular funerary practice nowadays in the UK.

65

Because a Welsh suffragist became the first female state senator in the USA and played a prominent role in advancing public health in the USA

Martha Maria Hughes was born near Llandudno, Caernarfonshire, in July 1857. The Hughes family were Mormons and chose to emigrate to Salt Lake City in the USA. She qualified as a medical doctor in 1880. In August 1884, she became the fourth wife of Angus Munn Cannon. He already had seventeen children by this time. This polygamy was against the law and Angus was sent to jail and Martha went to ground in England. While she was in England, Angus married two other women. Martha eventually returned to the States and, in 1896, Martha Hughes Cannon became the first woman elected as a state senator in the United States. She stood in Utah as a Democrat against her husband, a Republican, and she defeated him by 10,288 votes to his 8,054. She introduced three Bills in her first month in state senate that resulted in an 'Act Providing for Compulsory Education of Deaf, Dumb, and Blind Citizens'; an 'Act to Protect the Health of Women and Girl Employees', which required employers to give female employees something to rest on when they were not serving customers; and, an 'Act Creating a State Board of Health and Defining its Duties'. As a result of the third Act, she was appointed to Utah's first State Board of Health.

66

Because a determined elderly lady gave pioneering care to soldiers in the Crimean War and is now a role model for modern nursing

Betsi Cadwaladr was born near Bala in north Wales in 1789, one of sixteen children. Life expectancy at her time of birth would have been about 40. Her mother died when Betsi was but 5 years old.

Despite her unpromising start, Betsi turned out to be a self-willed and adventurous woman, travelling for years as the captain's maid on a ship, where she exercised her peculiar talent of performing Shakespeare. On her eventual return to Britain she decided to train as a nurse at Guy's Hospital, London. She qualified at the remarkable age of 65. In November 1854, she volunteered to serve as a military nurse in the Crimean War.

Betsi was posted to the hospital at Scutari where Florence Nightingale was in charge. They did not get on. Betsi was more of a free spirit, prepared to bend the rules to give bespoke care to injured soldiers. She then moved closer to the front line at Balaclava, and became famous for her battles against authority to acquire necessary supplies for her patients. She improved bedding, bandages and diet for the injured soldiers. She even broke the rules and spoke to the patients, and in a kindly way. She cooked, cleaned and nursed for up to twenty hours a day. Her health broken by dysentery and cholera, she came home and died in 1860. She was buried in a pauper's grave. She is sometimes known as 'the Welsh Nightingale' – although given her antipathy to Florence, Betsi would not have approved. Betsi's memory is honoured by the name of the Betsi Cadwaladr Health Board in north Wales, the largest health board in Wales. Today she is regarded as a great role model for nurses, not least in her battles against gratuitous authority and her advocacy on behalf of patients.

67

Because a Welsh girl from the Rhondda Valley became captain of Arsenal Ladies football team, winning them nine league titles while also playing for Wales sixty-one times

In 1979, Jayne Ludlow was born in Llwynypia in the south Wales Valleys. She showed an early talent in football and played with the local boys' team until the age of 12, when she was told that she would not be allowed to continue. There were no girls' teams in the Valleys at that time so she had to travel all the way to Barry to play there. She continued her career in London and ended up by playing for Arsenal, where her manager called her 'the best box-to-box player in the women's game'. She was voted Players' Player of the Year in 2001, 2003 and 2004. She rose to become captain of Arsenal and of the Wales national team. She played sixty-one times in all for Wales. She is Arsenal Ladies' highest scorer of all time, and won nine league titles, a UEFA Women's Cup and six FA Cups with the club. She retired from playing football in 2013 after her coach had described her as 'the most successful player that Wales has ever had'. Following her retirement from active football, she moved into management and became coach to the Wales national team between 2014 and 2021 and its youth teams. She was awarded an MBE in the 2019 Birthday Honours for services to women's football in Wales.

68

Because football's first superstar was a miner from north Wales

William (Billy) Meredith was born in 1874 in Chirk, a mining town in Denbighshire, Wales. He began work at Black Park Colliery as a pit pony driver at the age of 12. He spent eight years working as a miner. He showed a talent for football and first played for the Chirk first team in September 1892. He was talent-spotted by Manchester City and signed up with them in 1894. He captained the team at the remarkable age of 21, leading them to the club's first major honour, the 1904 FA Cup. He changed to play for Manchester United in May 1906 and won the league title in 1907–08 and 1910–11, the FA Cup in 1909, and two FA Charity Shields. He also helped to set up the Players' Union, which was a predecessor of the Professional Footballers' Association. He returned to Manchester City in 1921 at the age of 47 and played a further thirty-two games before retiring in 1924. He was the oldest ever player for City, United and Wales. In all, he gained forty-eight caps for Wales. Billy is considered to be football's first superstar, and he was nicknamed 'the Welsh Wizard'. He was inducted into the Football League 100 Legends in 1998 and the English Football Hall of Fame in 2007.

69

Because Welsh sporting personalities held world records

Ray Reardon was born in Tredegar in 1932. His first job as a miner did not work out too well. After being buried for three hours in a rock fall in the Florence colliery, he changed his career to that of policeman. He became a professional snooker player in 1967 and won the first *Pot Black* tournament in 1969. He also won the 1976 Masters and the 1982 Professional Players Tournament. Reardon was the dominating figure in snooker in the 1970s, winning the World Championship in 1970, 1973, 1974, 1975, 1976 and 1978. He was the first player to be ranked World Number One when world rankings were first introduced during the 1976–77 season, and he held that rank for five years. He regained the top-ranking position in 1982 and was awarded an MBE in 1985. Reardon retired as a professional in 1991 and is enrolled on the Roll of Honour of the Welsh Sports Hall of Fame.

Leighton Rees was born in Mountain Ash in 1940 and became a professional darts player in 1976. After twice winning the darts tournament on the Indoor League in 1974 and 1976, he won the World Cup singles in 1977 at Wembley. In 1978, he triumphed at the inaugural Embassy World Professional Darts Championship in Nottingham. In all, he won seventy-seven caps playing darts for Wales. Rees was a darts player who not only became best in the world but helped popularise the sport.

Lynn Davies was born in Nantymoel in 1942. He became a track and field athlete, specialising in the long jump. In 1964, he won an Olympic gold medal in Tokyo with a jump of 8.07m. For this he earned the soubriquet 'Lynn the Leap'. He became the first athlete to hold Olympic, European and Commonwealth titles at the same time. In all, he set seventeen British and Commonwealth records during his sporting career. He was twice BBC Wales Sports Personality of the Year and was awarded a CBE in 2006.

Colin Jackson was born in Cardiff in 1967 and showed early sporting prowess. He won a silver medal in 110m hurdles in the 1986 Commonwealth Games, and took the 110m hurdles silver at the 1988 Olympic Games. He set a world record for the 110m hurdles in August 1993, a record that stood for thirteen years, and won his first World Championships gold medal in Germany in 12.91 seconds. He set an indoor world record at the 60m hurdles with a time of 7.30 seconds in Germany in 1994 and he was the sole holder until February 2021. At the 1994 European Indoor Championships he became a double European champion by winning in both the 60m hurdles and 60m sprint race. His 60m dash time of 6.49 seconds was a European record, as well as a championship record. These records remained unbeaten for five years. Between August 1993 and February 1995, he won forty-four races consecutively. His winning time at the 1994 Commonwealth Games was a Commonwealth Games record. He was awarded a CBE in 2003.

70

Because the man recognised as the greatest rugby player of all time came from Gwaun-cae-Gurwen

Gareth Edwards was born in 1947 in Gwaun-cae-Gurwen (GCG) near Pontardawe. In a poll of international rugby players conducted in 2003 by *Rugby World* magazine, he was voted the greatest rugby player of all time (the highest ranking English player was twelfth). He is one of the few Welsh players to have won three Grand Slams. Some say he was the scorer of the greatest ever try when he played for Barbarians against the All Blacks in 1973, a game the Barbarians won by 23 points to 11. Edwards was central to the success of the Welsh rugby team in the 1960s and '70s. At the age of 20, he was Wales's youngest ever captain in February 1968 against Scotland, a game Wales won 5-0. Edwards won fifty-three caps for Wales, won five successive Triple Crowns, and scored twenty tries. He also won ten caps for the Lions and was part of the legendary 1971 team that won a series in New Zealand. He also played in the unbeaten 1974 side that toured South Africa. Edwards is self-deprecating but Will Carling, the former English rugby captain, said of him in 2007, 'He was a supreme athlete with supreme skills, the complete package ... He was outstanding at running, passing, kicking and reading the game.' Edwards was knighted in 2015 for services to sport and charity.

Wales is understandably proud of its rugby heroes. On 15 March 2008, Wales won the rugby Triple Crown for the second time by beating France 29 points to 9 in Cardiff's Millennium Stadium. Wales were crowned Grand Slam champions for the second time in four seasons. Wales also won the Six Nations Championship by beating England, Ireland, Scotland, France and Italy that year. The population of Wales in 2008 was 3 million; the population of Ireland in 2008 was 4.5 million; comparative figures for Scotland were 5.2 million, England 51.8 million, Italy 58.8 million, and France 64.4 million. So, for a nation with a population of that size to come out top of a league of nations with a combined total of 185 million is noteworthy.

71

Because Wales continually produces a crop of fantastic boxers, often emerging from difficult circumstances

'Peerless' Jim Driscoll was born in Cardiff in 1880. His father died in a works accident before Jim was 1, and he was brought up in extreme poverty. He began boxing in fairground booths to try to win prize money. After 600 such fights he turned professional and took the British Featherweight championship in 1906. He successfully defended his title in 1907 and won the Commonwealth title in 1908. He is a member of the International Boxing Hall of Fame. In 1925, 100,000 people lined the streets of Cardiff to watch his funeral.

Jimmy Wilde was born in Quaker's Yard in 1892. He started work down the mines at the age of 12. A miners' strike forced him to try to earn a living by boxing at the age of 16. By 1914, he had fought some 500 fights in boxing booths, often beating opponents far heavier than himself. One day in Pontypool he knocked over seventeen opponents before lunch and after a cup of tea knocked down another eight. He was rejected twice from enrolment into the British army as unfit during the First World War – he had a gammy leg and was underweight. In April 1916, Wilde won the IBU World Flyweight title. He retained the title until 1923. He is often rated as the greatest British fighter of all time, and the greatest flyweight boxer ever. He was the first official World Flyweight champion. His nicknames, such as the Mighty Atom, the Ghost with the Hammer in his Hand and the Tylorstown Terror, reflected his immense punching power. Wilde would take on bantamweights and featherweights and knock them out. He boasts the longest unbeaten streak in boxing history: he had 103 fights before his first loss. His record is 139 wins, three losses, one draw and five no contests, with ninety-nine wins by knockout. *Ring Magazine* rated him the third greatest puncher of all time. In 1990, he was elected to the inaugural class of the International Boxing Hall of Fame and, in 1992, the Welsh Sports Hall of Fame. He was ranked as the top flyweight of all time by the International Boxing Research Organisation in 2006.

Brian Curvis was a professional southpaw boxer from Swansea, born in 1937. He fought as a welterweight and was never beaten by any British boxer. He became British Welterweight champion in 1960 and held his title until 1966, when he retired. He is the only man to have won two Lonsdale Belts. He was BBC Wales Sports Personality of the Year in 1960.

Howard Winstone, the son of a rag and bone man, was born in Merthyr Tydfil in 1939. As a factory hand he lost the tops of three fingers of his right hand – not a good start for an aspiring boxer. Nevertheless, he went on to win eighty-three out of his eighty-six amateur boxing fights. By 1958, he was ABA Bantamweight champion. Representing Wales at the 1958 British Empire and Commonwealth Games in Cardiff, he won the Bantamweight gold medal. He turned professional in 1959, and won his first twenty-four fights in a row. In 1961, he boxed Terry Spinks at Wembley and won the British Featherweight title. By 1963, he had successfully defended this title three times, and crowned that achievement by winning the European Featherweight title, which he successfully defended seven times. In 1968, he won the World Featherweight title. He retired at the age of 29. *The Guardian* described him as 'one of the most talented boxers ever to grace a British ring'.

Joe Calzaghe was born in 1972, the son of a Welsh mother. His family lived on a council estate in Newbridge, near Caerphilly. He was bullied at school, and left there without qualifications. In 1993, he turned professional as a boxer and in October 1995 became British Super-middleweight Champion. In October 1997, he became the WBO Super-middleweight Champion by beating Chris Eubank. He was the longest-reigning Super-middleweight World Champion in the history of boxing, sustaining the WBO title for over ten years and defending it against twenty opponents (a record in the class) before moving up to light-heavyweight. Since his super-middleweight and light-heavyweight championships overlapped, he retired in 2009 with the longest continual time as world champion of any active boxer at the time. He was also the first boxer to hold three of the four major world titles (WBA, WBC, and WBO) at super-middleweight, and was the first ring champion in that division. He had fought forty-six professional fights and won all of them. He is ranked the second greatest European boxer of all time, but the greatest pound for pound. In 2006, Calzaghe was voted BBC Sports Personality of the Year. In 2014, he was inducted into the International Boxing Hall of Fame.

72

Because of a magical location that has inspired architecture, cult television, world-renowned pottery and steampunk

Portmeirion in north Wales has been named one of top 500 unmissable experiences in Lonely Planet's ultimate UK travel hitlist. It has a lot going for it – not least castles dating back to the twelfth century.

Then there is the inspiring architecture of Clough Williams-Ellis, who traced his lineage back to Owain Gwynedd, Prince of North Wales. In 1925, Williams-Ellis acquired the land that was to be home to his proposed ideal village. He wanted to show how a naturally beautiful location could be developed and the natural background enhanced through sympathetic development. With this vision, Portmeirion village was born and first opened in 1926 on Easter weekend. The Aber Iâ estate was ideal for his plan, with steep cliffs overlooking a wide sandy estuary, woods and streams as well as some old buildings. During the initial building work the most distinctive buildings were erected in an Arts and Crafts style and from 1954–76 he filled in the details. The second period was classical in style. Many of the buildings were salvaged from demolition sites. Today, Portmeirion is a popular hotel resort and tourist attraction with thousands of guests and day visitors every year. Be seeing you …

The village has been the inspiration for writers and television producers and film makers. Most notably, the enigmatic cult TV series *The Prisoner* was filmed here in the 1960s. The individualism the series promoted has an insidious appeal. Other programmes featuring Portmeirion include *Doctor Who*. The village has been used by pop groups and bands for music videos and is home to an annual arts and music event, Festival No. 6, named after the central character in *The Prisoner* played by Patrick McGoohan. The Portmeirion giftshop sells the very collectable and distinctive pottery designed by Susan Williams-Ellis, daughter of Clough Williams-Ellis. The pottery itself is now based in Stoke-on-Trent but Portmeirion remains its spiritual home. Portmeirion now also boasts the Portmeirion Steampunk weekend.

73

Because two men of Welsh descent were leading artistic lights in the nineteenth century

William Morris was born in March 1834, of Welsh descent on his father's side. He was friends with William Burges, the great rebuilder of Cardiff Castle. They were both medievalists and an influence on each other, and they had dreams of transporting themselves and others to a chivalric golden age. Morris painted, wrote novels, and designed furniture and textiles but he was best known in his day for his poetry. He translated poems from Icelandic, Anglo-Saxon, Greek and Latin. In 1891, he set up the Kelmscott Press, which printed fifty works, all expensive but beautifully illustrated. Nowadays, he is best remembered for his achievements in the decorative arts, notably in textiles, embroidery, wallpaper and stained glass. Some of his designs are still in production. He is considered to be the single most important figure in British textile production. The biographer of Morris claimed that his ethos was, 'have nothing in your houses that you do not know to be useful or believe to be beautiful'. He also described him as, 'a manufacturer not because he wished to make money, but because he wished to make the things he manufactured'.

In 1872, Morris published *Love is Enough*, a poetic drama based on a tale in the old Welsh *Mabinogion*. Both he and his friend Edward Burne Jones were very much influenced by the legends of King Arthur, with all the deep Welsh roots that they possess. His first volume of poetry was *The Defence of Guinevere* and his only surviving oil painting seems to be a portrait of Guinevere (Gwenhwyfar in the original Welsh – some say she is buried at St Elltyern's at Capel Llanilltern, west of Cardiff).

Edward Burne Jones was born in 1833 and was destined to become a leading light in the Pre-Raphaelite art movement. His father, Edward Richard Jones, was a Welsh frame maker. He met William Morris while studying at Oxford and they became good friends. Together they founded The Brotherhood at Oxford, which gradually expanded its membership and influence. Dante Gabriel Rossetti, founder of the Pre-Raphaelite Movement, befriended them both and described them as 'men of genius'.

Burne Jones went into business with Morris in an artistic firm that undertook carving, stained glass, carpets, metalwork, chintzes and paper hangings. Burne Jones was primarily known as a painter but he was also an illustrator, designing books for the Kelmscott Press. His paintings were seminal in the Aesthetic Movement. In his own words he described his Celtic romanticist approach, 'I mean by a picture a beautiful, romantic dream of something that never was, never will be – in a light better than any light that ever shone – in a land no one can define or remember, only desire – and the forms divinely beautiful.' His best painting is reported to be 'The Last Sleep of Arthur in Avalon'. His personal notepaper was headed 'Avalon'. Morris & Co. supplied Burne Jones's stained glass windows and ceramics for Llandaff Cathedral in Cardiff. Sir Edward Coley Burne-Jones (by then hyphenated) was knighted in 1894.

74

Because *The Voice UK* derives much of its popularity from its Welsh coaches and advisers

In March 2006, Tom Jones, son of a miner and born in a terraced house in Treforest, became a Knight of the Realm. For his first paid gig as a singer in 1957 he earned £1. He did not make it big until he recorded 'It's Not Unusual', which made No. 1 on St David's Day, 1965. A string of hits followed such as 'Delilah' and 'Green, Green Grass of Home'. Jones performed in Las Vegas from 1967 to 2011. He has sold over 100 million records in his career and has notched up thirty-six Top 40 hits in the UK and nineteen in the USA. He seems to have a remarkable gift for reinventing himself for new generations and, despite the bias of TV against persons 'd'un certain âge', he appears to have become an almost indispensable trainer on the annual series of *The Voice UK* from 2012 until now.

Jones had a hit with Cerys Matthews in 1999 with a version of 'Baby, It's Cold Outside'. In Series 1 of *The Voice UK* in 2012 Matthews appeared as an adviser to Jones's team. That series pulled in 10 million viewers. Jones has been the winning trainer three times so far in the series.

In 1999, Matthews sang with Catatonia at the colourful opening ceremony of the Rugby World Cup at the new Millennium Stadium in Cardiff. This event took place at the height of 'Cool Cymru' spearheaded by the Manic Street Preachers, Stereophonics and Catatonia.

Cerys Matthews was born in Cardiff but brought up in Pembrokeshire before she moved back to Cardiff, where she co-founded the band in 1992. Success followed with notable hits such as 'Mulder and Scully' and 'Road Rage', with Matthews's distinctive voice becoming a soundtrack for the time. Following the break-up of the band in 2001, Matthews reinvented her musical career as a solo artist, spending time in Nashville. Her career blossomed and she found increasing success with her studio albums, writing and broadcasting. She has appeared on Radio 2 and Radio 6 as well as presenting shows for television. Matthews received an MBE for services to music and continues to champion Welsh folk songs and Welsh music.

Kylie Minogue joined *The Voice UK* as a trainer in 2014 and returned as an adviser to Jones's team in 2018. She was born in Melbourne, Victoria, in May 1968 and is the highest-selling Australian artiste of all time. Her mother, Carol, is Welsh-born from Bridgend. Kylie is very much aware of her Welsh roots and has visited her Welsh-speaking grandmother in Cymmer. Kylie's 'lucky, lucky' partner, Paul Solomons, is Welsh, too. Kylie first shot to fame in *Neighbours*, an Australian version of *Pobol y Cwm*. But it is her career as a pop singer that has outshone her achievements as an actress. Her debut album, *Kylie*, released in 1988, topped the UK album chart in 1988 for six weeks, and two of its tracks, 'I Should Be So Lucky' and 'The Loco-Motion', have become classics of her repertoire. Her second album, *Enjoy Yourself*, hit No. 1 in the UK album chart in 1989 and remained in the top ten for sixteen weeks. Kylie has now sold more than 80 million records worldwide. In 2020, her album *Disco*, reached No.1 in the UK, and she is the first female artist to have released No. 1 albums in five decades, from the 1980s to the 2020s – a tribute to her ability to reinvent herself – just like Tom Jones – in music and fashion over the years.

75

Because 'the sexiest woman of the twentieth century' who has had seven decades of top 40 hits was born in a rough part of Cardiff

Shirley Bassey, the daughter of an illegal immigrant, was born in a terraced house in Butetown in Cardiff in 1937 at a time when Butetown was the wrong side of the tracks. Her first job was packing enamel utensils. By night she would sing in pubs and clubs. In 1959, she achieved a hit parade No. 1 with 'As I Love you', the first Welsh person to top the pop charts. She was to go on to sing the title track of three James Bond movies: *Goldfinger*, *Diamonds are Forever* and *Moonraker*. In 2008, she was inducted into the Grammy Hall of Fame for her recording of 'Goldfinger'. In both 1972 and 1973, *TV Times* voted her Best Female Singer. In 1998, a Welsh newspaper poll voted her the 'Sexiest Woman of the Twentieth Century'. Wales was to export her singing talent to the world. She was a great hit on the Las Vegas stage, and she has even won the French Légion d'Honneur in 1999. In 2019, she was accorded the freedom of her home city of Cardiff. In 2020, she became the first female artiste to have a top 40 album in seven consecutive decades. She has sold more than 140 million records worldwide and has had twenty-seven hits in the UK

Top 40. On 19 July 2000, 'Cardiff's Tigress from the Bay', was made a Dame of the British Empire at Buckingham Palace. In 2023, the Royal Mail announced that Dame Shirley Bassey would be honoured with a commemorative stamp issued on 21 September 2023 – she is the first female artiste to be so honoured.

76

Because the world's most successful classical singer of this century proudly flies the flag for Wales

Katherine Jenkins was born in Neath in June 1980. She entered a modelling competition and became the 'Face of Wales 2000', but she decided to launch a musical career. On the strength of an audition, Universal Classics and Jazz offered her a six-album deal – the most lucrative in the UK's classical recording history and reportedly worth £1 million. On 5 April 2004, the mezzo-soprano released her first album, *Première*, which hit No. 1 on the UK classical music charts. Six months later, her second album, *Second Nature* also reached No. 1 and was followed by her first win of the Classic Brit Award for Best Album in 2005. Six out of seven of her studio albums reached No. 1 in the UK classical charts between 2004 and 2008, selling a total of more than 4 million copies. She effectively became the world's most successful classical singer after Classic FM announced her as 'the Biggest Selling Classical Artist of the Century' in 2017. Fourteen of her albums have reached No. 1 – an all-time record in itself. In 2005, Jenkins became the official mascot for the Wales rugby union team. She was awarded an OBE in the 2014 New Year Honours for her services to music and for charitable service. She is an ambassador for the cancer charity Macmillan and a trustee of the British Forces Foundation.

Jenkins has A-level Welsh and can sing in the language. She was married in Cardiff Castle. In an interview she gave in 2014, she said, 'I love Wales in such an enormous way. No matter where I am in the world, I always try and fly the flag.' In 2022, she launched her own gin, Cygnet Gin, distilled in Swansea and made with the purest Welsh water.

77

Because one of the world's biggest investors in tech industries is Welsh

Michael Moritz was born in Cardiff in 1954. He started out as a journalist and wrote a book about the early history of Apple, managing to offend Steve Jobs in the process. Then he became a venture capitalist, specialising in hi-tech start-ups. His investment in Google made him one of Wales's richest men in 2004. He made legendary successful bets on Yahoo and PayPal, too. He was to become the No. 1 listing in Forbes's Midas List of the top 100 dealmakers in the technology industry in 2006, and on 23 March 2016 Forbes asked 'Who's Been on the Midas List More than Anyone?' The answer was Moritz – he had appeared in it for fifteen years. Forbes stated, 'Apart from this year's No. 28 rank, Moritz has been consistently in the top 20 for a decade and spent 6 years straight (2006–2011) at either no. 1 or no. 2.' In June 2008, he made a donation of $50 million to Christ Church, his former Oxford college – the largest donation in the college's history. In July 2010, he was awarded an honorary fellowship at Cardiff University, where his father had been vice-principal and Professor of Classics. He was knighted in 2013.

78

Because the first billionaire in Wales turned his birthplace into an internationally renowned five-star resort

Terry Matthews was born in Newport in south Wales at the Lydia Beynon Maternity Hospital in 1943. He studied electronics at Swansea University. His first enterprise, Mitel, a manufacturer of small PBX systems and microprocessors, was bought out by BT in 1985. After re-acquiring Mitel, he sold it again in 2018 for $2 billion. He became a serial entrepreneur, establishing over 100 technology companies, and he was the first man to become a billionaire in Wales. In 1986, he founded Newbridge Networks and sold it to Alcatel in 2000 for $7.1 billion. Intriguingly, he bought the old maternity hospital he was born in, renovated its central manor house and invested £100 million in it. Matthews was to comment: 'I think the resort can act as a magnet to draw new investment into Wales from across the UK and overseas. I did my best to put up a building that you can see from the West End of London and I didn't come far short of it!' The five-star Celtic Manor Resort does indeed dominate the skyline at Newport and is internationally renowned. In 2014, the resort hosted the NATO summit. That resort alone is said to be worth £3.5 billion. In 2001, Matthews was knighted for services to Wales and to industry.

79

Because UNESCO sees the slate landscape in north-west Wales as a 'model for other slate quarries in different parts of the world' and as 'a remarkable example of interchange of materials, technology and human values'

Slate was mined in north-west Wales since Roman times – indeed the Romans used slate as roofing in their fort at Segontium, near Caernarfon. The slate landscape of north-west Wales was awarded UNESCO World Heritage status in July 2021. Between 1780 and 1940, the Welsh slate industry dominated world production of roofing slates. By the late nineteenth century, this area produced a third of the world output of roofing slates and architectural slabs. Its use in terraced houses, factories, warehouses and elite architecture contributed to rapid global urbanisation. The mines pioneered revolutionary technologies, including ingenious applications of waterpower, bulk handling systems and the first known application of the circular saw for cutting stone. These technologies were spread by specialists and by the emigration of skilled Welsh quarrymen to the developing slate industries of the USA, continental Europe and Ireland. The narrow-gauge railway systems – which remain operational to this day – used to carry away the slate to new coastal ports inspired similar systems worldwide and were adopted from Asia and America to Africa and Australasia. Llechwedd's deep mine opens to the public for tours, and you can travel 500ft into the mine on the steepest cable railway in Europe. Penrhyn remains the world's largest producer of high-quality slate.

80

Because UNESCO rates a Welsh aqueduct as 'a masterpiece of creative genius and a remarkable synthesis of expertise already acquired in Europe'

The Pontcysyllte Aqueduct in north-eastern Wales was declared a World Heritage site by UNESCO in June 2009. On its completion, this 11-mile length of canal was described as 'composed of works of more difficult of execution than can perhaps be found anywhere within an equal distance of canal navigation'. It was designed by the civil engineer Thomas Telford.

The aqueduct is an eighteen-arched stone and cast iron structure designed for use by narrowboats and was completed in 1805, having taken ten years to design and build. It is 12ft wide, is the highest canal aqueduct in the world and the longest aqueduct in Great Britain. The mortar used contained ox blood – a cheap way to fortify mortar exposed to freeze–thaw temperature cycles. The aqueduct carries the Llangollen Canal across the River Dee in the Vale of Llangollen. For some 130 years of its initial use, it carried traffic in coal, iron, slate, limestone and general goods. The canal has now become one of the most popular canals for holidaymakers in Britain because of its aqueducts and scenery. The aqueduct is now maintained and managed by Glandŵr Cymru.

81

Because UNESCO describes Blaenavon as 'one of the prime areas of the world where the full social, economic and technological process of industrialisation through iron and coal production can be studied and understood'

The Blaenavon area illustrates the pre-eminence of south Wales as the world's major producer of iron and coal in the nineteenth century and its role in the Industrial Revolution. All the necessary elements still exist – coal and ore mines, quarries, a primitive railway system, and the social infrastructure of the community. The central focus is usually on the six Blaenavon blast furnaces where pig iron was produced between 1789 and 1902. It is the best-preserved blast furnace complex of its period in the world. Nearby is the Big Pit National Coal Museum, a coal mine that opened in 1860 and operated until 1980. In 1878, Sidney Gilchrist Thomas and Percy Gilchrist invented at Blaenavon the Basic Bessemer process, which was of worldwide importance in permitting phosphoric iron ores to be used in bulk steelmaking. Visitors can explore all the ancillary buildings around the ironworks: the cast houses, boiler rooms, engine houses, the water balance tower for hoisting and lowering railway trucks, and the three ranges of workers' housing forming Stack Square. These houses have been refurnished to show how people lived in the eighteenth, nineteenth and twentieth centuries. In December 2000, the Blaenavon industrial area became a UNESCO World Heritage Site.

82

Because UNESCO regards four large castles in north Wales as 'Europe's most ambitious and concentrated medieval building project'

Wales boasts the highest density of castles of any nation in the world. One prominent contributory reason is that it took the Normans four years to conquer England but they had difficulty in overwhelming the Welsh since 'Ei gwrol ryfelwyr' ('its manly warriors') presented more of a challenge. Indeed, three Royal Houses later, the Plantagenets were still facing an uphill struggle.

If you drive around large parts of north Wales, the impression is of expanses of windblown, woolly farmland, tranquillity and human sparsity. But, suddenly, turn a corner and a colossal castle confronts you, bespeaking the wealth and determination of the man who built them. Six castles built by Edward I form an encompassing ring around north-west Wales.

Some Welsh Nationalists have a negative attitude to these castles, regarding them as monuments to their subjection by the English. Those promoting Welsh tourism often used to be a mite diffident about exploiting the castles' image. But are they right to despise their magnificence in this way? Those who disdain these Edwardian castles should instead look at them as healthy tokens of the resilience of nationhood, admire them for their quality, and use them to attract more tourism to Wales.

One of the most basic lessons about archaeology is that man is lazy: he takes the path of least resistance; old trackways tend to be the quickest routes from A to B; men tend to source their raw materials as closely as possible to the site of construction. Similarly, if castles are built proudly, grandly and expensively, then there must have been a purpose to them. Surely, in the thirteenth century the population density must have been even thinner than the crowded twenty-first century? The population of Wales under Edward was about one tenth of what it is now. Why were these medieval monsters built so laboriously to hold down the peripheral, thinly scattered rural Welsh?

They are truly fine creations. Four of them are UNESCO World Heritage sites. The castles have been described as, 'Europe's most ambitious and concentrated medieval building project'.

Edward I stayed in Rhuddlan for some time. The castle is moated on three sides, and on the fourth the River Clwyd affords protection. The river is straightened and deepened to allow ships to deliver goods direct from the sea in case of siege.

By using the 'Way of the Sea', a path of 108 steps, Harlech Castle could be supplied from the sea. It successfully withstood a siege by Madog ap Llewelyn.

Edward I continued a castle rebuilding programme begun by his father, Henry III, in Wales. However, the six great castles that he built in north Wales were his own creation. The first five were built to try to prevent yet another expensive military campaign against the Welsh. In 1277 and 1282, Llewellyn had risen against the English Crown and the core of his resistance was in Snowdonia and Anglesey. Their building must be a tribute to the robustness of the Welsh resistance; and if they were intended as a prophylactic measure they failed because the Welsh arose again in 1294 when the castles were nearly complete. In *A History of Wales*, John Davies comments, 'The conquest did not lead to the assimilation of the Welsh by the English.' This is despite the fact that bastide towns with protective walling were established outside the castles of Flint, Caernarfon and Conwy, and were effectively plantation towns populated with English settlers: no Welshman was even allowed inside the bastides. If a Welshman was found in the bastide after sunset he could be hanged. Beaumaris was begun in 1295 after the third revolt.

The first two to be built were Flint and Rhuddlan, both begun in 1277. Flint has a fairly simple design with a square court and three-quarter round towers, and its stone keep has walls a massive 23ft thick; in the south-east it has a strong, detached round tower. Rhuddlan boasts a court in a diamond shape, two impressive gatehouses and corner towers. Edward's later castles show an evolution in concept with the usage of concentric design so that inner defences can bring to bear firepower from arrow loops and crenellations.

Conwy, Harlech, Caernarfon and Beaumaris were all designed by Master James of Saint George d'Esperanche, a master military architect. Edward spent a great deal of money on his castles, some £80,000, many times his annual income. At times money was tight. In 1296, Master James wrote, 'The work we are doing is very costly and we need a great deal of money ... For God's sake be quick with the money

Built in just four years between 1283 and 1287, Conwy is magnificently preserved and boasts the most intact set of royal apartments in Wales.

Caernarfon Castle.

for the works ... Otherwise, everything done up to now will have been of no avail.' In 1299, unpaid workmen were threatening to abscond. Building took place mainly between April and November. The castles absorbed large workforces, often from far away. In 1287, about 2,500 workers were employed on Caernarfon, Conwy and Harlech; in 1295, Beaumaris had 3,000 men working on it. All the castles were built with direct access to the sea and supplies – a recipe that worked well in their defence during the second uprising.

Master James's creations all show similar styles to the castles he built in Savoy. They tend to have broadly square wards, large gatehouses and round corner towers. Caernarfon is more distinctive, reflecting its intended use as the main seat of English power in north Wales. It has polygonal towers and turrets. Its main gate has no fewer than

Beaumaris has four concentric rings of formidable defence and its outer walls have 300 arrow loops. The moat has its own dock.

six portcullises. With Caernarfon's towers being banded and decorated with eagles, some see similarities with the Theodosian Wall of Constantinople. Edward was perhaps trying to make the point that Caernarfon, so close to the Roman Fort at Segontium (a Roman stronghold that passed into Welsh legend), represented the western border of Roman imperium just as Constantinople represented the eastern. Caernarfon Castle reflected the imperial glory of Rome on Edward's empire. Conwy was built above the tomb of Llewellyn the Great – no doubt more concrete symbolism. Conwy Castle is placed in an excellent strategic position.

The building of these castles marked the end of the period of the castle as a prime military instrument. That they were virtually outdated is shown by the fact that Beaumaris was never finished. From this period on, castles were really semi-fortified homes rather than strongpoints to hold down territory. Warfare was increasingly becoming a matter of movement. It could even be that these castles were built as much for show as for military ends. Within a generation, the major castles were manned by no more than a dozen soldiers and the smaller castles were unmanned.

Michael Prestwich, in his work *Edward I*, comments, 'There was no immediate need to build on the scale of Caernarfon or Beaumaris and the English can hardly have expected the Welsh, once conquered, to develop military capabilities they never had when independent.' His thesis is that the 'ever increasing ambitiousness of the castles' is unrelated to political or military requirements but reflects the artistic impulse of Master James to make each successive creation more splendid than his last.

So, there are two broad interpretations of the real reason for the creation of the castles: either Edward wanted to project symbols of his power so that the Welsh would look upon his works and despair; or Master James craftily expended his employer's money in pursuit of ever more grandiose personal creations for posterity to admire. A practical and efficient means of subduing the Welsh they were not. For instance, in 1404, the Welsh Prince, Owain Glyndŵr, captured Harlech Castle, made it his military headquarters and held a parliament there in 1405.

The main thrust of a history of Wales, *Aros Mae* (There still remains), written by that veteran Welsh Nationalist Gwynfor Evans, is that despite all the anglicisation and subjection of Wales there remains a sense of separate identity and pride in Wales. This feeling found its expression eventually in the creation of the Welsh Assembly in 1999. If Edward planned to extirp Welshness by means of his constructions, he singularly failed.

Edward II's biographer wrote of the Welsh that 'according to the sayings of the prophet Merlin they will one day repossess England'. That writer of rich English prose, Owen Rhoscomyl, described the Welsh Tudor Henry VII coming to the throne of England as, 'The long struggle over, the victory won.' In this sense, the castles are a reminder of how transient power can be.

83

Because the archaeology of Wales entices us with its secrets still to spill

The Prince of Wales Orthopaedic Hospital in The Walk in Cardiff was formally opened by the then Prince of Wales in 1918. It was founded to help heal limbs shattered in the First World War. The driving force behind it was Sir John Lynn-Thomas, the orthopaedic revolutionary (see Reason 61). Intriguingly, this building, now demolished, featured a megalithic monument near its entrance. The megalith haunts the memory, but it has vanished, too. It was not old, but modern: it was placed there by Sir John Lynn-Thomas, who had a fanciful passion for Welsh archaeology. He cast his spell to echo for decades to come.

Just as the substrate of Welsh intonations and grammar structure often breaks through into monoglot English speakers in Wales today; just as Celtic moodiness and mysticism marinate everyday life in Wales, so, too, does the rich history of human habitation in Wales suffuse into our lives, sometimes through written scripts, folklore and legend and, sometimes, through archaeology.

Archaeology in Wales has its own history. In 1823, Dean William Buckland, otherwise known for his eccentric eating habits (including, for instance, moles and bluebottles), discovered in a cave on the Gower Peninsula the ochre-stained bones of a human that he named 'the Red Lady of Paviland'. His sexing of the bones was incorrect – later studies showed that these were the bones of a young man. Buckland dated the remains to Roman times but again he was wrong. The bones have been dated to 31,000 BC; they are the earliest known modern human found in the UK. When the Red Lad was alive this cave was not on the coast but 70 miles inland and overlooked a plain to the west. These lost lands are reflected in folk legends of a sunken lost kingdom off the west coast of Wales, Cantre'r Gwaelod.

Glyn Daniel was born in Lampeter Velfrey, Pembrokeshire, in 1914. He won a scholarship to Cambridge and graduated in Archaeology and Anthropology with first class honours and a distinction. He continued his academic career at St John's College, Cambridge. His archaeological interests centred on megaliths and prehistoric tombs, but his lectures in Cambridge majored on eccentric aspects of archaeological history. He took particular delight, for instance, in telling the story of Archbishop Ussher, who by meticulous study of biblical genealogies concluded that God created the world on 22 October 4004 BC at six o'clock in the afternoon (hence, Petra in Jordan, which is 3,000 years old, is in John Burgon's poem, a 'Rose-red city, half as old as time').

Daniel's affable and eccentric personality made him a natural for TV and radio. He hosted the TV series *Buried Treasures* for the BBC in the 1950s. In this role, he played a large part in popularising archaeology for the modern viewing audience. It was a baton to be picked up by the archaeological series *Time Team*, which ran from 1994 to 2014.

Time Team covered several fascinating Welsh digs. A 1994 episode featured an excavation of a crannog on Llangorse Lake near Brecon, a man-made island in a lake. It is the only crannog known in England and Wales as they are most closely associated with Ireland. Legend associates the area with King Brychan of Brycheiniog (Breconshire), himself of Irish origin. The dig discovered a high-status tunic, maybe a diplomatic gift from the House of Wessex (perhaps King Alfred) to a Welsh king who had sworn fealty in exchange for protection. Other indicators of royal status are the immense amount of human labour that must have been invested in building the crannog and the bridge to it; deer bones reflecting a royal passion for hunting; the remains of a reliquary; and, other items indicating the ownership of horses. The crannog's construction was dated to AD 89, and the dig found evidence that the crannog had been destroyed by fire. The *Anglo-Saxon Chronicle* tells that in AD 916 Queen Aethelflaed of Mercia (eldest daughter of Alfred) 'sent an army into Wales and destroyed Brecenanmere (Llangorse Lake), and captured the king's wife and 34 other persons'. The archaeology fits the written record.

In 2009, *Time Team* broadcast its dig in Caerwent (Venta Silurum), the best-preserved Roman settlement in Britain. Its impressive stone walls stand up to 17ft tall with towers that would have been capable of siting a ballista atop. Caerwent had public baths, a temple and a large forum with basilica and the team found a high-status villa with heated baths, and shops. The local tribe, the Silures, had resisted the Romans for up to thirty years but were finally pacified in about AD 75 and bought into the Roman way of life, with planned towns, and central heating, Roman administration and dress. Tacitus, the Roman historian, described how the Romans civilised former barbarians:

> Hence, too, a liking sprang up for our style of dress, and the toga became fashionable. Step by step they were led to things which dispose to vice, the lounge, the bath, the elegant banquet. All this in their ignorance they called civilisation, when it was but a part of their servitude.

The Time Team televised its dig at Caerleon in 2012. Caerleon is named after the Roman fortress established there, 'castra legionis' (the fortress of the legion). The 2nd Augusta Legion built the encampment in about AD 75, and it was occupied by legionaries until about AD 300 –

it is one of the longest sustained occupations of a fortress in the whole of the Roman Empire. The site was partly chosen to try to hold down the restive Silures. The fort covered 51 acres and it is estimated that 370 acres of woodland had to be felled to construct it. The extensive baths complex would have needed to be heated by wood collected from 13,800 acres of woodland. The amphitheatre outside the fortress is well preserved – it is 184ft long and 136ft broad and its wooden seats would have had the capacity to seat the whole legion. The team discovered warehouses and port facilities that would have been vital to keeping this legion supplied: the River Usk is tidal to this point – doubtless another reason why the fort was sited here.

The team covered 'Copperopolis' in 2012. Copperopolis was the nickname given to the Swansea area because of its vast concentration of copper smelting – it was once the copper capital of the world. There was no copper in the area but what it had were abundant supplies of coal for coal-fired reverberatory furnaces: Swansea also had a fine port on the River Tawe for ocean-going vessels to bring in the copper ore and export the smelted high-quality metal. By the 1830s, Swansea accounted for 90 per cent of the copper smelting capacity in Britain and by the 1860s it accounted for 65 per cent of the world's output of smelted copper. From the 1780s, widescale copper sheathing was used by the Royal Navy and this gave it a big fighting edge, and an increase in speed of some 20 per cent, so Swansea was vital in the growth of empire and in the Navy's success against the dictator Napoleon. The skills acquired by local copper smelters were also exported around the world, which perhaps explains why there are twenty-six Swanseas around the world and very few Cardiffs.

The archaeology of Wales strains to be unearthed to illuminate the present. A cornucopia of truths begs to be disinterred. We have the seven halls of the first university of Europe at Llantwit Major lost to sight (see Reason 4). Shifu Careaga of the University of Kentucky locates Camelot in Thornhill, north of Cardiff at a hillfort called Caer Melyn, so far undisturbed by an archaeologist's trowel.

Then there is the mysterious Castle Morgraig. *The Discovery of the Ark of the Covenant*, a book published in 2007, locates the Ark in Wales and as part of its quest it cites Castle Morgraig on the outskirts of Cardiff. Cadw, the Welsh equivalent of English Heritage, labels the castle as 'odd'. Although the remains are substantial, it was not rediscovered until the twentieth century. Most Cardiffians are unaware of the castle, hidden in a clump of trees near the Traveller's Rest pub on Caerphilly Mountain. It stands on the historic division between Senghenydd and Glamorgan and its strongest defensive wall faces south towards what was then Norman-dominated Glamorgan. One legend associated with this strangely shaped construction is that it is the 'Welsh Alamo' where a Welsh rebellion was defeated in 1315. However, no one knows who built it or why. The castle, like so many subterranean structures in Wales, keeps its secrets … so far.

84

Because Stonehenge may be a recycled monument first erected in Wales

UNESCO designated Stonehenge as a World Heritage Site in 1986. Yes, this prehistoric monument is in England, but there are grounds to believe that it is a recycled monument that was first erected in Wales some centuries previously (probably 3,300 BC). The research by Professor Mike Parker Pearson and his team at UCL Institute of Archaeology was published in *Antiquity* on 7 December 2015. The paper indicated that the 'bluestones' in Stonehenge were made of dolerite quarried in the Preseli region of Wales – more than 175 miles away. They were erected in the first phase of Stonehenge's construction (c.3,050 BC–2,950 BC). In 2018, an excavation at the Waun Mawn stone circle discovered six sockets of removed stones. Waun Mawn would have had the same alignment towards the sun on Midsummer's Day and the same diameter as the ditch surrounding Stonehenge. It looks like the western Welsh may have taken some of their sacred stones with them to Wiltshire and re-erected them there; the stones have acoustic properties and ringing them may have played a carillon (a tune produced by a musical instrument of the same name) – sounds from home. About 15 per cent of the people buried at Stonehenge when the bluestones were erected there probably came from west Wales, according to isotopic analysis of cremated bones. How did these crafty old Welsh transport at least forty-three of these stones weighing 2 to 4 tons each over a distance of 175 miles? It must have been a remarkable technological challenge.

85

Because an eighteenth-century Welsh painter is known as 'the father of British landscape painting'

Richard Wilson was born in Penegoes, a village in Powys, in 1714. He studied art in London, where he began to earn a living by portrait painting. Then he went to study in Venice and from there to Rome. It was in Italy that he was advised to concentrate on landscapes rather than portraiture. In 1757, he returned to London and to the peak of his career in expressing romantic emotion within a classical framework. He concentrated on classic Italian landscapes, Welsh landscapes and landscapes of rural areas around London. He exhibited at the Society of Artists from 1760. He was a founder member of the Royal Academy in 1768 and its librarian from 1776. Towards the end of his career his popularity took a dip – it may have been connected with a decline in his health and personality. He died in poverty in 1782 in Denbighshire in Wales. However, he was to inspire the painters Turner and Constable. Nowadays, Wilson is regarded as 'the Father of British Landscape Painting'. The National Museum of Wales has fourteen of his paintings and the Yale Centre for British Art in New Haven, Connecticut, boasts one of the largest Wilson collections in the world, including a landscape of Caernarfon Castle.

86

Because an 'electric mountain' in north Wales provides green energy to the UK grid at times of surging demand

In May 1984, Charles, the then Prince of Wales, opened Dinorwig Power Station at Llanberis in Snowdonia. The power station makes use of green hydro-electric energy. Although it is difficult to store energy, essentially this plant acts as a giant battery. Electricity powered by hydro generated at periods of low demand is used to pump a large amount of water from a lake, Llyn Peris, up the mountain (Elidir) to a reservoir storage (Marchlyn Mawr), then to be released to generate electricity at periods of high demand or to manage sudden surges in demand (for instance during television commercial breaks – electricity grid managers pay a good deal of attention to TV schedules). Dinorwig is known locally as Electric Mountain, and when it opened it was regarded as the world's most imaginative engineering and environmental project. It is still the largest scheme of its type in Europe. The turbine hall, also known as the Concert Hall, is also Europe's largest man-made cavern. Its six turbines can produce a maximum of 1,727MW and can power up in as little as sixteen seconds. Its storage capacity is 9.1GWh. The plant cost £425 million to build and it represents the largest civil engineering project by value ever awarded by a UK government at the time.

87

Because a mid-Wales town with 2,000 inhabitants became the largest second-hand and antiquarian book centre in the world

Hay-on-Wye is a rather sleepy border town in mid-Wales. It once had a reputation for its hostelries. For a town with about 2,000 inhabitants, thirty-four public houses at one time seem a lot. In 1962, Richard Booth bought a second-hand bookshop there and in doing so began to change the image of the town. He began buying stocks of books big time, shipping them in by the ton from America and elsewhere. Eventually, he expanded to seven bookshops in Hay. On 1 April 1977, he paraded through the town centre proclaiming himself 'Richard Coeur de Livres', king of the independent country of Hay. His horse was appointed prime minister and he arrogated to himself the right to nominate hereditary peers of his nation thereafter. His cabinet meetings were held monthly in one of the remaining local hostelries. By the late 1970s, Hay was known as the 'Town of Books'; by the 1980s, it boasted some thirty bookshops. Although this number has fallen, Hay is still the largest second-hand and antiquarian book centre in the world.

Booth claimed that he led the Independent Kingdom of Hay out of the European Union (or the EEC as it then was) in 1978, blazing a trail for the UK to do likewise in 2020. Despite his insurrection, he was awarded an MBE in the 2004 New Year Honours List. Although not a great businessman himself, Booth did a tremendous amount for books, Hay and tourism in Wales. The 'Town of Books' was the inspiration for the annual Hay Festival.

In 1988, Hay-on-Wye held its first International Festival of Literature and Arts, which was founded by the Florence family. This event grew like Topsy. The annual star-studded festival attracts some 500,000 tourists annually. In 2001, Bill Clinton called it 'the Woodstock of the mind'. Imitative sister festivals take place all around the world. In April 2009, the Hay Festival won the Queen's Award for Enterprise.

88

Because the craft of Welsh whisky distilling once exported to the USA has revived itself in Wales in the multi-award-winning Penderyn Distilleries

Whisky distilling was a traditional Welsh craft from the fourth century that had died out by 1903 when the Frongoch distillery closed. In 2004, Penderyn whisky was launched upon the world: Charles, the then Prince of Wales, was at the launch. With that, whisky distilling was back in Wales after a gap of at least 100 years. Penderyn was chosen as the site for the distillery because it possesses its own source of natural spring water. Penderyn now exports to more than forty countries around the world. A second distillery opened in Llandudno in May 2021, and a third Penderyn distillery opened in Swansea in July 2023 after an investment of £15 million. Penderyn Royal Welsh Single Malt Whisky won the Gold Medal Award at the IWSC 50th Anniversary Awards Banquet in 2019. Penderyn won six Golds and a Commended (in World Distiller of the Year) in the New Wizards of Whisky Awards 2022. Penderyn's gin, rum, and vodka have all won many awards, too.

The restoration of this lost art in Wales is heartening because it appears that the know-how was essentially exported to America by emigrant Welsh distillers. For instance, the Evan Williams family had a distillery in Pembrokeshire in 1705 but emigrated to the New World and founded the Kentucky bourbon industry. Evan Williams Bourbon is rated by many connoisseurs to be the finest of all bourbons. Jack Daniels is acknowledged as having a Welsh ancestry: in 2012, a businessman claimed to have found the original recipe in a dusty old book in Llanelli.

89

Because the greatest European legend is based on the exploits of a Welshman

Many people agree that King Arthur was a Romano–Celtic warrior fighting against the incursions of the Saxons and Picts after the departure of the Romans. This enhances the claim by some Welsh people that they are 'sons of the Romans'.

His history has been overlaid by myth and romanticisation. It is impossible to disentangle fact from fable. Should this man, the greatest of all European legends, even be considered Welsh? His name is Welsh – Bear Man. The first mention of him is in 'Y Gododdin', a Welsh poem from the sixth century where a warrior kills 300 men, but the poem dismisses him as 'no Arthur'. The Isle of Avalon (Welsh for apples) may correspond to Bardsey Island, where the stricken Arthur was taken after his final battle. The island's former name was Ynys Afallach. Some attribute Merlin's burial place to Bardsey. Arthur is also mentioned in the Welsh Triads from the sixth century. In Welsh, England is Lloegr; in Arthurian legend England is referred to as Logres. It all adds up to a reasonable argument that Wales endowed us with the rich mythology of Arthur, Camelot and Merlin.

Arthur and Merlin may well not be just simple legends. They are Welsh creations and may be in part Welsh history. On 24 February 1152, Geoffrey of Monmouth was created Archbishop of St Asaph. From a variety of sources Geoffrey composed his *Historia Regum Britanniae* (The History of the Kings of Britain), *Prophetiae Merlini* (Prophecies of Merlin) and *Vita Merlini* (The Life of Merlin). These three books are in themselves seminal sources of all the tales, mysteries and romantic mythology surrounding King Arthur and his wise adviser, Merlin. He places Carmarthen (the Fort of Merlin) as the birthplace of the magician. The Historia Regum Britanniae describes Arthur's successful battles against the marauding Saxons and then his conquests of Ireland, Iceland, Norway and Gaul. Then Arthur saw off an army of resurgent Romans but eventually he was brought down after a battle with his evil nephew, Mordred, in his final stand at Camlan. Arthur was 'mortally wounded' but curiously was carried away to the Isle of Avallon 'to be cured of his wounds' – some date this to AD 518. One legend has it that Arthur left Cardiff Castle on his final journey and that one day he will return when his country is in mortal danger. If so, Cornish people and Bretons will be disappointed because many of them hope for his resurrection and return.

The Arthurian legends are brimful of Celtic mysticism, romance, betrayal, chivalric warfare, good battling evil, and a mysterious quest for the Grail (one contender being the Nant Eos cup). All these are intriguing ingredients that make and remake enchanting stories. Because they are so multi-layered, conflicting and probably a pick and mix of truth and fiction, each generation can reshape them so that they strike contemporary chords or reinvent themselves. Various parts of Britain – and Europe – can claim him as their own.

Terry Breverton, Welsh writer and lecturer, has him as a warlord from Glamorgan and Gwent who may have spent his final years as a Welsh emigrant to Brittany. Norman Davies, the historian, prefers to place him in the proto-Welsh speaking area of Strathclyde with his fortress at Dumbarton Rock – or 'Castrum Artori', as it was known to antiquaries. He acknowledges other claims to Arthur's home as being Roxburgh and Glasgow.

Breverton claims that the book *Journey to Avalon – the Final Discovery of King Arthur*, 'makes a persuasive case that Arthur's court ... was Llanmelin hillfort, the ancient capital of the Silures, that overlooks Caerwent Roman town'. Nennius, writing in the eighth century, placed Arthur's ninth battle at Caerleon. Geoffrey of Monmouth claims that Arthur held a magnificent court at the City of the Legions (Caerleon) in 'the magnificence of the royal palaces with lofty gilded roofs that adorned it'. Others have Camelot sited at Caer Melyn, north of Cardiff, Dinas Powys Fort or Cadbury Castle in Somerset.

Various places have a claim to be Arthur's burial place. Gerald of Wales has him buried in Glastonbury. Walter Map, writing in the twelfth century, claims that Arthur was buried in the Black Chapel of Blackfriars Friary in Bute Park, Cardiff.

90

Because the heart of Cardiff's once derelict docklands has turned into an upmarket pleasure ground with the 'best theatre built in the world in the last fifty years'

The Docklands of Cardiff once had such a rough reputation that it was said the local police would not stray into the area on weekends, but would venture in on Mondays to retrieve the bodies. The Cardiff Bay Development Corporation was established in April 1987 to regenerate 2,700 acres of largely derelict docks and slums with its mission, 'to put Cardiff on the international map as a superlative maritime city, which will stand comparison with any such city in the world, thereby enhancing the image and well-being of Cardiff and Wales as a whole'.

Today the centrepiece of the project is the Millennium Centre in Cardiff Bay. It won Gold Medal for Architecture at the National Eisteddfod of Wales in 2005. The centre boasts a large theatre (2,497 seats) and two smaller venues with shops, bars and restaurants. It houses a total of eight arts organisations. A world-class arts centre located in Cardiff Bay had been planned for many years. The Cardiff Bay Development Corporation had supported an opera house, curiously resembling a glass box. Although attracting world-class architects for its design competition, it failed to win financial support from the Millennium Commission. The new plan also struggled with funding but plans were boosted by large donations from South African businessman Donald Gordon and a loan from HSBC. The construction of the centre started in February 2002 and Phase 1 opened in November 2004. It was built at a cost of £106 million. The architectural concept was to express 'Welshness', and the building was constructed with local Welsh materials from different parts of Wales such as slate, metal, wood and glass. Two lines from the poet Gwyneth Lewis are inscribed on the front of the dome above the main entrance. This lettering, 'In these stones horizons sing' is illuminated at night, as is 'Creu Gwir Gwydr O Ffwrnais Awen' (Create truth from the furnace's breath).

The completion of the centre has provided a home for the Welsh National Opera and allowed large London musicals such as *Les Misérables* and *Mary Poppins* to be successfully staged. The centre is now a much-cherished addition to the Cardiff Bay landscape, offering a wide range of diverse entertainment for all ages along with shops, bars and restaurants.

For Lord Lloyd Webber the centre is the 'best theatre built in the world in the last 50 years'.

Cardiff's Millennium Centre.

91

Because the 2nd Marquess of Bute set Cardiff's port on a trajectory to outshine Liverpool and eclipse Newcastle

The 2nd Marquess of Bute was an irritable, arrogant and penny-pinching man but he was a canny and far-sighted investor. He followed the 1st Marquess's desire to aggrandise his family. In this he certainly succeeded, built what became the greatest coal port in the world and stimulated the whole economy of south Wales. He set out to make Cardiff more important than Liverpool. His plan was to triumph: Cardiff eclipsed Newcastle as well.

The plan was strategic leveraging of his vast land holdings in south Wales. Cardiff would become a bustling port; this would raise his portfolio of ground rents. It would stimulate further investment by ironmasters and coal owners. The iron and coal would stream out of the port in exports, elevating his dock revenue and mineral rights. He expected his greatest return from coal. Using his own money, the 2nd Marquess obtained a Parliamentary Bill to give him powers to build a dock. The first stone was laid in 1837 and the dock opened on 8 October 1839. At a time when the town's population was barely 10,000, an impressive crowd of some 15,000 people marched from Cardiff Castle to the West Bute Dock for the occasion. At the celebratory dinner at the Cardiff Arms Hotel, the Mayor paid tribute to the Marquess for his 'munificence' in providing the means whereby posterity could transport 'their treasure from their hills to foreign lands' – the 2nd Marquess had invested £250,000 in dock building. Previously, the conveyance of iron and steel from the Valleys down to Cardiff had been restricted to the narrow Glamorgan Ship Canal. Foreign exports of coal from Cardiff grew steadily from 20,000 tons in 1845 to 7,500,000 tons in 1900. The Marquess's investment sparked a whole series of other investments in railways and docks that made Cardiff rich and provoked a population explosion (the population of Cardiff in 1831 was 6,187; by 1901 it had risen to 164,333). The investment, however, had not made the 2nd Marquess rich. His expenditure on the Glamorgan Estate exceeded his income and on his death in 1848 he left a son only 6 months old and debts totalling £493,887.

92

Because the 3rd Marquess rebuilt two ruinous castle piles into fairyland extravaganzas, eventually to devolve to the citizens of Cardiff

The trustees of the 2nd Marquess were empowered by his will to carry on with dock building and they and the 3rd Marquess, when he came of age in 1868, carried on with the investment. East Bute Dock, Roath Dock and Queen Alexandra Dock all expanded Cardiff's handling facilities. They created a thriving port that at its peak in 1913 was exporting 13 million tons of coal and the Coal Exchange Building in Cardiff was setting the worldwide price of coal. It was opened in 1886. As *The Western Mail* proudly pointed out at that time, 'There was a telephone attached to the building.' This building is thought to be where, in 1904, the world's first million pound business deal was done.

The 3rd Marquess was not his father. His father was Protestant, practical, pompous and parsimonious. The 3rd Marquess was Papist, painfully shy, polite and philanthropic. He was to bequeath a shining jewel to the people of Cardiff – or rather two jewels: he rebuilt Cardiff Castle and Castell Coch in Tongwynlais. He was able to do this partly because his father's investments had matured, and the 3rd Marquess was reputedly the richest man in the world. Another reason why he was able to endow Cardiff was that he became friendly with

The Cardiff Coal Exchange, which used to set the worldwide price of coal.

the Gothic architect William Burges. The 3rd Marquess was so shy that he longed to retreat into a mystical medieval world – and Burges was able fully to indulge him. Burges turned an antiquarian ruin 'in a disgraceful state of filth and ruin' into a suitable seat for the Marquess, now Mayor of Cardiff. He began by erecting a commanding clock tower in the south-west corner of the castle between 1869 and 1871. It dominated the skyline of Cardiff and afforded a silhouette of the castle as, in J. Mordaunt Crook's words, 'an explosion of archaeology and romanticism'. Burges wove his eclectic magic throughout the castle and Crook's overall verdict was that the rooms were 'fantasy capsules, three-dimensional passports, to fairy kingdoms and realms of gold. In Cardiff Castle we enter a world of dreams.' These rooms are now open to the public, and they represent an artistic feast for the contemporary visitor at the heart of the city.

Banqueting Hall, Cardiff Castle – great to hire for a party.

Despite a sniffy comment of a National Trust visitor in 1944 that the residence was 'the most hideous building I have ever seen', we prefer the judgement of the castle historian, Matthew Williams. The castle is, 'a colourful feudal extravaganza, bright with stained glass, painted murals and decoration'.

The 3rd Marquess entrusted the rebuilding of Castell Coch to Burges as well. Here he was starting with less than at Cardiff – the decaying debris of Gilbert the Red's thirteenth-century castle to protect the Taff Valley from the Welsh. Burges rebuilt it between 1875 and 1879. The result is an enchanting castle with echoes of *Sleeping Beauty*. Once again, the restoration was all paid out of the Marquess's own pocket. According to Cadw, the result is 'a dazzling masterpiece of the High Victorian era'. It is regularly voted by the public as their most favourite building in Wales.

In 1947, the 5th Marquess of Bute gave Cardiff Castle to the people of Cardiff and in 1950 he gave Castell Coch to the Ministry of Works.

93

Because the 4th Marquess of Bute is known as 'the man who saved Caerphilly Castle'

Caerphilly Castle covers 30 acres: it is the largest castle in Wales, and second only in size to Windsor across the UK. The ruined castle eventually came into the possession of the Bute family in 1776. From 1928 until the start of the Second World War the 4th Marquess of Bute restored all the collapsed parts of the castle. Cadw, the Welsh heritage body, calls his generosity, 'The biggest, most thorough and most authentic project of its type ever undertaken in Britain.' In this, he was following the antiquarian instincts of his father. Just like his father, he spoke Welsh fluently, was of a philanthropic bent and was motivated by social concerns. Caerphilly's local economy was suffering the aftereffects of the General Strike of 1926. For twelve years, he employed fifteen full-time masons along with large numbers of labourers and contractors. By 1936, he had spent more than £100,000 of his own money – and the castle as visitors admire it today is largely down to him. In his honour there is a statue of him appearing to hold up the famous, slighted Leaning Tower of the castle. The 5th Marquess of Bute presented the castle to the state in 1950.

94

Because Wales has produced some of the best male voice choirs in the world

The Fron Male Voice Choir was founded in 1947 to compete in the Llangollen International Musical Eisteddfod. It is based in the village of Froncysyllte, close to Llangollen in north Wales. The population of Froncysyllte is 606, so it was not going to be easy to assemble a team of sixty members (the minimum necessary). But, they did it. They had to wait thirty years before the choir won at Llangollen in 1977. The same year they won the National Eisteddfod of Wales, thus completing 'the Double'. In 1998, the choir won the Gold Medal at the Athens International Choral Competition. In 2018, seventy years after first competing in the Llangollen International Eisteddfod, the Fron Choir took the prize for Best Male Voice Choir, reclaiming the International Trophy for Male Voice Choirs they had first donated to the competition in 1971. Their recorded album, *Voices of the Valley*, was released in November 2006 and reached No. 9 on the UK album chart. It became the fastest-selling classical record of all time, achieving gold status in three days and, by 2009, it had sold more than 500,000 copies.

The origins of the Treorchy Male Voice Choir go back to 1883 when a group of local lads sang 'Myfanwy' at the Red Cow Hotel and won the prize of £1 for their efforts. The choir formalised over time and its reputation grew to the extent that they were summoned for a Royal Command Performance at Windsor Castle before Queen Victoria in November 1895. The choir reformed after the Second World War on 16 October 1946. Throughout the 1950s and '60s the choir enjoyed a 'realm of gold', competing in national Eisteddfods. They won twenty-two first prizes out of twenty-seven entries. The choir has made more than fifty commercial recordings. In October 1984, BBC4 announced that the Treorchy Male Voice Choir had been voted among the top three choirs in the world. In November 2005, it gave a Royal Command Performance at the Wales Millennium Centre. Sir Anthony Hopkins says of the choir, 'As a Welshman that can't sing, I never feel more proud to be Welsh than when I hear the Treorchy Male Choir – the Master Choir of them all.'

95

Because the first and only Welsh man to become prime minister is widely credited with winning the First World War and laying the foundations of the modern welfare state

On 10 April 1890, David Lloyd George was elected Liberal MP for Caernarfon and at 27 years old he was the youngest Member of the House of Commons at that time. His ability and oratorical powers were soon recognised and by 1908 he had become Chancellor of the Exchequer. He introduced old age pensions in 1908 and National Insurance against illness and unemployment in 1911. As such, he was the progenitor of the modern welfare state. Lloyd George became Minister of Munitions in 1915 to address the political scandal that had broken out that May regarding a shell shortage on the Western Front. He succeeded in this, and the output of munitions rose to prodigious levels. Dissatisfaction with the laid-back prime minister, 'squiffy' Asquith, propelled Lloyd George to the premiership of a coalition government on 6 December 1915. As prime minister, he eventually managed to introduce an overdue convoy system to protect merchant shipping in April 1917 – an innovation essential to keeping the nation fed. Sinkings by German submarines declined after the adoption of convoys. He also set up a War Cabinet that met daily to promote the efficient running of the war. He brought his skills as a political operator to the job, such that he earned the nickname 'the Welsh Wizard'. His contribution to the War Cabinet was an infectious dynamism and a deep understanding of the way ordinary people lived and worked. So, as prime minister, he presided over the successful prosecution of the First World War, albeit at an immense cost in blood and treasure. Winston Churchill delivered the verdict on him: 'The greater part of our fortunes in war and peace were shaped by this one man ... He was the greatest Welshman which that unconquerable race has produced since the age of the Tudors.'

96

Because an uneducated Welshman is recognised as a nineteenth-century pioneer in factory reform, the father of distributive co-operation and the founder of nursery schools

Robert Owen, the son of a postmaster, was born in Newtown, in Montgomeryshire, in May 1771. He was destined to make striking advances in working conditions, education and industrial reform in Britain. He received very little formal education and became an apprentice draper at the age of 10. It was in the cotton mills in New Lanark that he reached his apogee as pioneering manager.

His plans for educating his workers included opening an Institute for the Formation of Character at New Lanark in 1818. Owen believed that character was moulded by the environment, so improving the work and home environment would lead to an improved society. He vigorously supported factory legislation that culminated in the Cotton Mills and Factories Act of 1819, which regulated the hours of work and moral welfare of young children employed in cotton mills.

He housed his employees in a model village with improved housing and sanitation, and provided medical supervision. The schools he provided took children from 3 to 13 in some cases. He was thus the founder of infant schools in Great Britain. He replaced the infamous and exploitative truck shops with co-operative shops where goods were sold to workers only a little above cost price. He adopted the principle of restricting a working day to eight hours. At a time when other mill owners were employing children as young as 5, he raised the minimum age of employment to 10. These reforms resulted in a more contented and efficient workforce and his enlightened capitalism resulted in greater net profit for the enterprise.

In 1825, Owen addressed the US House of Representatives. He imparted to them his vision of paternalistic employers and utopian communities. In fact, the utopian settlements he founded in the USA, such as New Harmony in Indiana, were not a long-term success.

The father-in-law of one of the authors of this book is named after this landmark social reformer.

97

Because algebra, the = sign and π were introduced to Britain by Welsh mathematicians

Robert Recorde arrived in this world in 1510 in Tenby. This clever young man went up to All Souls College, Oxford, where he became a fellow. He later qualified as a Doctor of Medicine at Cambridge and was official physician to both Edward VI and Mary Tudor. However, it was as a mathematician that he was to become famous. Essentially, he introduced algebra to Britain. One of his books on arithmetic went into fifty editions and another to twenty-six. In one of his books, *The Whetstone of Wytte*, he was to introduce the = sign to 'avoid the tedious repetition of equals to'. He was also Comptroller of the Bristol Mint from 1549 to 1551. His last post was as Surveyor of Mines and Monies in Ireland but after failure of the silver mines in Wexford he found himself in jail for mismanagement – a sad end for a brilliant mind. He introduced the word 'Zenzizenzizenic' as the eighth power of a number, but this did not catch on.

P.S. Besides the Welsh origin of =, the origin of π owes itself to another Welshman, William Jones from Anglesey in 1706.

98

Because a Welsh man became President of Madras and was the prime benefactor of one of the most prestigious universities in the world

The ancestry of Elihu Yale tracks back to Chancellor Thomas Yale, born in 1525, to many Welsh royal and noble houses as descendants of the Royal House of Mathrafal, the Royal House of Aberffraw, the Princely House of Powys Fadog, and the Tudors of Penmynydd. Elihu was born in Boston, Massachusetts, but left America at the age of 3 and never returned. He led a somewhat picaresque life, being President of Madras while in the employ of the Honourable East India Company. Yale died in 1721 and is buried in St Giles's churchyard in Wrexham after being elected as High Sheriff of Denbighshire. In 1718, the New England clergyman Cotton Mather had contacted Yale to seek his help on behalf of the Collegiate School of Connecticut, which needed money for a new building. Yale sent Mather 417 books, a portrait of King George I and nine bales of goods. These were sold by the school for £800. In recognition of his generosity, the new building was named Yale; eventually the entire institution became Yale College. Yale University is the third-oldest institution of higher education in the USA and is among the most prestigious in the world. It has produced sixty-five Nobel laureates and five US presidents.

99

Because a Welsh man was the one person on the planet to make this world more secure between 1990 and 2003

David Kelly was born in 1944 in Llwynypia in Glamorgan. He was appointed to the United Nations Special Commission in 1991 as one of its chief weapons inspectors in Iraq and led ten of the organisation's missions between May 1991 and December 1998. He also led several missions to Iraq by its successor body, the United Nations Monitoring, Verification and Inspection Commission. Tony Blair's Labour government had issued a notorious 'dossier' in 2002 that stated some of Iraq's chemical and biological weapons were deployable within forty-five minutes. David Kelly had an off-the-record meeting with a journalist, Andrew Gilligan, in 2003. During that meeting, Gilligan gained the impression that Kelly thought the 'forty-five minute' element was overegging the pudding in order to justify the invasion of Iraq. Gilligan appeared on BBC Radio 4's *Today* programme and was interviewed by Cardiff-born John Humphrys. Gilligan essentially accused Alistair Campbell, Blair's Director of Communications, of sexing the dossier up by insisting on the inclusion of the forty-five-minute claim. An almighty row blew up between the BBC and the government. Kelly was eventually fingered as the source of the accusation and was interrogated in an aggressive manner by a Select Committee. On 17 July 2003, Kelly was found dead in the countryside near his home (this was two days after a Select Committee grilling). Official verdicts thereafter deemed his death a suicide. Norman Baker, a former Minister of State in the coalition government of 2010–15, who wrote a biography of Kelly, had this to say of him, 'It is no exaggeration to say that between 1990 and his death in 2003, Dr Kelly probably did more to make the world a more secure place than anyone on the planet.' Michael Howard, a Welshman from Llanelli, who led the Conservative Party between 2003 and 2005, believes Kelly was murdered.

100

Because the 'greatest Englishman who ever lived' had Welsh roots and was born in Wales

In 1888, 'T.E. Lawrence' was born illegitimately in Tremadog on the Lleyn Peninsula. His mother's mother was Welsh. This man, born in Wales with Welsh roots, imbued with the Welsh characteristics of romanticism, moodiness and secretiveness, was destined to be labelled – ironically enough – by historians as 'the greatest Englishman who ever lived'. He won the Welsh Meyricke scholarship to study history at Jesus College, Oxford (Edmund Meyricke, a Welsh cleric, who died in 1713, bequeathed funds for scholarships to aid promising Welsh-born students at Jesus). Thereafter, Lawrence became an archaeologist working in the Middle East. He was swiftly recruited by British Military Intelligence to undertake a secret survey of the Negev Desert, an important, geographically strategic area in the British struggle against the Ottoman Empire in the First World War. From 1916, he played a very active part in encouraging the Arab Revolt against the Ottomans, with many successful raids culminating in the capture of the strategic town of Aqaba on the Red Sea. In 1926, his fine autobiographical account of his daring exploits, *Seven Pillars of Wisdom*, was published under his name. Winston Churchill thought that it ranked with the greatest books ever written in the English language.

In his later years, Lawrence was employed in the Royal Air Force as an aircraftsman working on high-powered motorboats. He had sought a certain anonymity, feeling that something was 'broken in the works' inside him. Lawrence, who was living under the pseudonym T.E. Shaw, was killed in a motorcycle accident on 19 May 1935. Churchill wrote of him, 'I deem him one of the greatest beings alive in our time … We shall never see his like again. His name will live in history. It will live in the annals of war … it will live in the legends of Arabia.' Three films and more than seventy biographies have been written about Lawrence of Arabia.

BIBLIOGRAPHY

Antiquity, 7 December 2015.
Breverton, Terry, *100 Great Welshmen*, Glyndwr Publishing, 2005.
Breverton, Terry, *An A to Z of Wales and the Welsh*, Christopher Davies (Publishers) Ltd, 2000.
Breverton, Terry, *The Book of Welsh Saints*, Glyndŵr Publishing, 2000.
Breverton, T.D., *The Welsh Almanac*, Glyndwr Publishing, 2002.
British Medical Journal, 16 July 1960.
Butler, Chris, *Cardiff Mysteries Remastered*, 2nd Edition, Amazon, 2021.
Careaga, Shifu, 'Caer Melyn (Camelot) – Cosmic Hillfort of the King: The Yellow Hill (fort) as a Cosmic Hill or mountain motif and symbol of a King's authority', May 2019.
Cohen, Susan, *Medical Services in the First World War*, Shire Publications Ltd, 2014.
Davies, John, *A History of Wales*, Penguin, 2007.
Davies, John, *Cardiff and the Marquesses of Bute*, The University of Wales Press, 1981.
Davies, Norman, *Vanished Kingdoms*, The Penguin Group, 2011.
Esquire, February 2003.
Diffie, Bailey W.; Winius, George D., *Foundations of the Portuguese Empire 1415–1580*, University of Minnesota Press, 1977.
Evans, Gwynfor, 'Aros Mae …', Gwasg John Penry, 1971.
Evening Standard, 6 March 1993.
Finch, Peter, *Edging Cardiff*, Seren Books, 2022.
Gramich, Katie, *The Works of Gwerful Mechain*, Broadview Press Ltd, 2018.
McKinty, Alec, *The Father of British Airships*, William Kimber & Co Ltd, 1972.
Montagu, Ewen, *The Man Who Never Was*, The Camelot Press Ltd, 1953.
Mordaunt Crook, J., *William Burges and the High Victorian Dream*, Frances Lincoln Ltd, 2013.
Mortimer, Dic, *A–Z of Cardiff*, Amberley Publishing, 2016.
Penn, Thomas, *Winter King*, Allen Lane, 2011.

Picture Postcard Monthly, October 2001 (permission was obtained from the then proprietors for repeating much of Chris Butler's article in this magazine in Section 82).
Prestwich, Michael, *Edward I*, Yale University Press, 1997.
Roberts, Alun, *Welsh National Heroes*, Y Lolfa Cyf., 2002.
Roderick, Alan, *The Dragon Entertains*, Wales Books, 2000.
The Cardiff Times, 13 August 1910.
The Daily Mail, 19 November 1967.
The Guardian, 22 April 2017.
The Independent, 3 April 2015.
The Scotsman, 21 April 2005.
The Spectator, 13 September 2014.
The Story of Food, Dorling Kindersley Ltd, 2018.
The Sunday Times, 26 July 1998.
The Western Mail, 2 February 1886.
The Western Mail, 3 January 1936.
Thorpe, Lewis (trans.), *Gerald of Wales*, Penguin Classics, 2004.
Wallechinsky, David; Wallace, Irving, *The People's Almanac*, Doubleday & Co. Inc., 1975.
Weekly Mail, 9 October 1896.
West, Nigel, *Churchill's Spy Files*, The History Press, 2018.
Williams, Jac L. (ed.), *Detholiad o Farddoniaeth Gymraeg* Christopher Davies Cyf., 1977.
Williams, Matthew, *Cardiff Castle and the Marquesses of Bute*, Scala Arts and Heritage Publications Ltd, 2019.
Wilson, A.N., *After the Victorians*, Arrow, 2006.
Wilson, A.N., *The Elizabethans*, Hutchinson, 2011.
Wilson, Alan; Blackett, Barum, *The Discovery of the Ark of the Covenant*, Trafford Publishing, 2007.
Zaczek, Iain, *Essential William Morris*, Dempsey Parr, 1999.

INDEX

Numbers in **bold** indicate 'Reason' number.

Actors
    Burton, Richard **23**, 55–6
    Gruffudd, Ioan **22**, 53–4
    Hopkins, Antony **26**, 61–2
    Jason, David **25**, 60
    Lewis, Damian **22**, 53–4
    Pryce, Jonathan **26**, 61
    Rickman, Alan **24**, 57–8
    Thomas, Gareth **13**, 39
    Zeta-Jones, Catherine **25**, 59–60
Adams, Sam – instigator of the Boston Tea Party **55**, 122
Angel Hotel, its use as a ship in First World War **9**, 30–1
Anglesey Sea Zoo **44**, 99
Archaeology **83**
    Caer Melyn, a possible Camelot 180
    Caerleon, legionary fortress 178, 191
    Caerwent Roman settlement 178, 191
    Castle Morgraig, Caerphilly's mystery castle 180
    Copperopolis, Swansea as 'the Copper Capital of the World' 179
    Crannog on Llangorse Lake 177–8
    Daniel, Glyn – Professor of Archaeology, University of Cambridge 177
    'The Red Lady of Paviland' 176–7
    Time Team 21, 177–8
Architects
    Jones, Inigo **46**, 102
    Myddleton, Hugh **46**, 103
    Nash, John **46**, 102–3
    Wright, Frank Lloyd – Welsh roots of **45**, 100–1
Ashley, Laura – fashion icon **54**, 111–2
Aviators
    Frost, Bill – airman who beat the Wrights to the skies **34**, 75
    Willows, E.T. – the 'Father of British Airships' **34**, 75–8

Battles **7, 35**
    Agincourt 27–8
    Bosworth 79
    Crécy 26–7
    Poitiers 27
Bevan, Aneurin **3**
    creation of NHS 18–9
    tribute paid to him by the BMJ 18
Booth, Richard – King of Hay **87**, 185–6
Boxers **71**
    Calzaghe, Joe 150
    Curvis, Brian 149
    'Peerless Jim Driscoll' 148
    Wilde, Jimmy 148–9
    Winstone, Howard 149

Cadwaladr, Betsi – role model for modern nursing **66**, 140
Cardiff Docklands **90**, 192–5
Chartism **28**, 65
Christianity in Wales **4**
    Faith in the Dark Ages 20–1
    Llantwit Major, site of first Christian university in Europe 21, 179
Coal Exchange **92**, 196–7
Comedians **57**
    Rob Brydon 127
    Tommy Cooper 126–7
    Bob Hope 126

Davies, Hugh Morriston – pioneer of war surgery **63**, 137
Davies, Russell T. – screenwriter and producer **13**, 39–40
Decorative artists **73**
    Jones, Edward Burne 153–4
    William Morris 153–4
Dee, John – Elizabethan polymath, court astrologer and astronomer **54**, 120–1
Dinorwig Power Station **86**, 184

Explorers
    Cabot, John and naming of America **53**, 118
    Prince Madoc, discoverer of America **54**, 120–1
    Scott, Robert Falcon – the Cardiff connection **52**, 113–7

Gerald of Wales, views on incest **39**, 89
Great Orme, prehistoric copper mines **48**, 106

Griffith, David Llewelyn Wark – 'Pioneer of Cinema' **58**, 128

Halen Môn, World's Best Ingredient **44**, 99
Hay-on-Wye – the 'Town of Books' **87**, 185–6
Heffer, Simon – claims the Welsh were civilised by the English **4**, 20
Holy Grail **50**, 109–10
Hughes, Martha Maria – pioneer of public health in the USA **65**, 139

Inventors
    Bowen, Edward, inventor of airborne radar **12**, 36
    Brunt, David, inventor of 'FIDO' **12**, 37
    Curran, Joan, inventor of 'window' **12**, 37
    Davies, Donald Watts, inventor of packet switching **16**, 45
    Davies, Tom and Walter, inventors of spare tyres **21**, 51
    Grove, William, inventor of the fuel cell **15**, 43–4
    Hooley, Edgar Purnell, inventor of Tarmac **21**, 52
    Hughes, David, radio transmission in 1879 and inventor of the teleprinter **19**, 48–9
    Marconi, Guglielmo, radio transmission in Wales in 1897 **19**, 48
    Pryce-Jones, Pryce, inventor of mail order and sleeping bags **19**, 47

Roberts, Larry, pioneer of ARPANET **16**, 45
Vaughan, Philip, inventor of ball bearings **15**, 43
Wingfield, Walter, inventor of tennis **17**, 46

Jenkins, Karl – classical composer **47**, 104–5

Kelly, David – weapons inspector **99**, 209–10
King Arthur **83**

Locations suggested for Camelot **83**, 180, 191
   Welsh legend? **89**, 189–91
Lawrence, T.E. – dubbed 'greatest Englishman who ever lived' **100**, 211–2

Male Voice Choirs **94**
   The Fron 201
   Treorchy 201–2
'Manly Warriors' of Wales **6**
   Victoria Crosses **6**, 23–5
   Welsh archers in the Hundred Years' War **7**, 26–8
   Weston, Simon **8**, 29
Michael, Glyndwr – role in Operation Mincemeat and 'the Man Who Never Was' **11**, 34–5
Marquesses of Bute
   2nd Marquess of Bute, creation of Cardiff as a leading port **91**, 194–5
   3rd Marquess of Bute 196–9
   4th Marquess of Bute, saving Caerphilly Castle **93**, 200
   Pioneer of viticulture in the UK **59**, 129–31
   Rebuilding two fairyland castles – Cardiff and Castell Coch **92**, 196–9
Mathematics $-$, $=$ and ϖ pioneered by Welshmen **97**, 207
Morgan, William – 'the Father of Modern Actuarial Science' **20**, 50
Morris, Robert – founder of the American financial system **53**, 119

Nation, Terry **13**
   creator of the Daleks 38
   scriptwriter for *Blake's 7* 38–9
   scriptwriter for *Doctor Who* 38
Nobel Prizewinners
   Evans, Sir Martin (Medicine) **14**, 42
   Granger, Clive (Economic Sciences) **14**, 42
   Josephson, Brian (Physics) **14**, 41
   Russell, Bertrand (Literature) **27**, 63–4
Nott, David – 'the Indiana Jones of Surgery' **62**, 136
Novello, Ivor – achievements of **2**, 17

Orthopaedics
   Founder of the Prince of Wales Orthopaedic Hospital, Cardiff **3**, **83**, 114, 176
   Thomas, Evan – bonesetter **61**, 134
   Thomas, Hugh Owen – 'the Father of Modern Orthopaedics' **61**, 134
   Jones, Sir Robert **61**, 134

Lynn-Thomas, Sir John **52**, **61**, **83**, 114, 134–5, 176p
Pioneer of the Thomas Splint in the First World War **61**, 134–5
Pioneer of Orthopaedics as a speciality **61**, 135
Owen, Robert – pioneer of factory reform **96**, 205–6
Owens, Arthur – agent SNOW and the 'Double Cross' system **10**, 32–3

Patagonia, Welsh settlement of **29**, 66–7
Poets
  Aneirin **42**, 96
  Cranogwen **37**, 82–5
  Davies, W.H. **38**, 86–7
  Gwilym, Dafydd ap **39**, 88
  Mechain, Gwerful **39**, 88
  Thomas, Dylan **40**, 90–1
Politicians
  Bevan, Aneurin **3**, 18–9
  Evans, Gwynfor **36**, 81, 175
  George, David Lloyd **95**, 203–4
Portmeirion – architecture, steampunk, pottery and cult TV **72**, 151–2
Price, William – the eccentric doctor who legalised cremation **64**, 138

Quant, Mary – fashion icon **51**, 111

Roberts, Joseph – founder of Liberia **5**, 22

Serial Entrepreneurs
  Matthews, Terry **78**, 162
  Moritz, Michael **77**, 161

Singers
  Bassey, Dame Shirley **9**, 30, **75**, 157–8
  Jenkins, Katherine **76**, 159–60
  Jones, Sir Tom **74**, 155
  Matthews, Cerys **74**, 155–6
  Minogue, Kylie **74**, 156
Sportsmen and Sportswomen
  Davies, Lynn – Olympic Gold Medallist for the long jump **69**, 145
  Edwards, Gareth – greatest rugby player of all time **70**, 146
  Jackson, Colin – World champion hurdler **69**, 145
  Ludlow, Jayne – Wales's most successful football player **67**, 142
  Meredith, William (Billy) – football's first superstar **68**, 143
  Reardon, Ray – World No. 1 snooker player **69**, 144
  Rees, Leighton – World champion darts player **69**, 144

Tudors
  Elizabeth I **54**, 92, 120–1
  Henry, Earl of Richmond, later Henry VII **7**, **35**, 79–80, 93, 175
  Henry VIII **50**, 109, 130
  Owen Tudor **7**, 28

UNESCO World Heritage Sites
  Blaenavon iron and coal production **81**, 166
  Edward I's castles in north Wales **82**, 168–75

Pontcysyllte aqueduct **80**, 165
Slate landscape of north-west Wales **79**, 163–4
Stonehenge, and its Welsh connections **84**, 181–2
US presidents of Welsh descent **56**
   Adams, John 123–4
   Adams, John Quincy 125
   Coolidge, Calvin 123
   Garfield, James 123
   Harrison, Benjamin 123
   Harrison, William Henry 123
   Jefferson, Thomas 124
   Lincoln, Abraham 123
   Madison, James 124
   Monroe, James 125
   Nixon, Richard 123
   Obama, Barack 123

Viticulture in Wales **59**, 129–31

Wallace, Alfred Russel – 'Father of Biogeography' **43**, 98
Welsh banking **60**, 132–3
Welsh gold **49**, 107–8
Welsh language
   Amerinds speaking Welsh **54**, 121
   growing bilingualism **42**, 95
   links with Breton and Breton onion sellers **42**, 97
   origins in Scotland and modern echoes of it **42**, 96, 190
   predating English **40**, 96
   Young, Toby – views on Welsh vowels **42**
Welsh Saints
   multiplicity of **4**, 20–1
   St David **4**, 21

St Joseph of Arimathea **50**, 109–10
St Patrick **4**, 21
Welsh whisky, revival of **80**, 178–80
Wilson, A.N.
   admiring Aneurin Bevan as the 'British MP who … did the most good' **3**, 19
   admiring John Cowper Powys as 'the greatest English novelist' **1**, 15
   critical of Welsh achievement **1**, 15
Wilson, Richard – 'the Father of British Landscape Painting' **85**, 183
Writers
   Dahl, Roald **33**, 73–4
   Davies, Andrew Wynford **32**, 71–2
   Lewis, Saunders **42**, 95
   Llewellyn, Richard – author of *How Green Was My Valley* **30**, 68–9
   Morris, Jan **31**, 70
   Shakespeare, William – Welsh connections and influences **41**, 92–3

Yale, Elihu – benefactor of Yale University **98**, 208